A GREAT WEEKEND IN

NAPLES

NAPULÈ MILA COLORI

'Naples of the thousand colours' is in some ways the 'enfant terrible' of Italian cities. With its unruly atmosphere and vivid contrasts, it's anything but a museum city. Its extroverted street-life and bright sunshine, deep shadows and dark secrets, make it the liveliest Italian city of them all. From the citrus yellow of Sorrento lemons and the turquoise waters round Capri to the ochre yellow of aristocratic palaces built of volcanic materials, and from the fuchsia pink of bougainvilleas to Vesuvius's dark silhouette, the thousand colours of the song are everywhere to be seen. Irresistible, inimitable Naples is there for you to experience rather than simply see.

Naples' favourable geographical location meant that it quickly became a popular tourist resort – as shown by the many aristocratic Roman villas found along the coast and on the islands. As you visit places like Pompeii and Sorrento, you'll easily understand the enchantment felt by travellers in the 18th century, when the region was one of the high points on the 'Grand Tour', attracting artists and

intellectuals from all over Europe. Yet there is far more to Naples than is shown in the static though harmonious images of the Bay of Naples seen in so many paintings and postcards, and far more also than the stereotypical trio of Vesuvius, mandoline and pizza (though each has its place). The main reason for this is that Naples hasn't yet been overrun by mass tourism and so still belongs to its inhabitants. Against the sumptuous backdrop of the Bay of Naples, Neapolitans go about their daily business, often with more than a hint of theatricality, as if they were making sure that outsiders only saw what they wanted them to see. This theatricality can be seen, too, in many of the traditions of the city that are likely to surprise the first-time

visitor, such as the San Gennaro miracle, the various processions that take place throughout the year, the small kitsch altars found on the walls of so many streets, the incongruous sound of the *zampogna* (a kind of bagpipe) at Christmas, and the *tarantella* dances improvised on the piazzas. But it would be a mistake to suppose that these are in any way mere relics of the past. On the contrary, such events and symbols are usually proof that certain

religious and secular rites have survived

and adapted to the times. Indeed, football heroes are just as much objects of veneration these days as the city's numerous saints. The liveliness and sudden changes of pace form a vivid contrast to the rhythm of other more ordered, less enticing Italian cities. If you really want to

get the feel of Naples and its surroundings, try not to pack too much into your visit. Rather than rushing from one place of interest to the next, take your time, linger and absorb, wander along alleyways and step into intriguing courtyards as the fancy takes you. As you'll soon discover, the city is a blend of various historical eras, including traces of the original Greco-Roman settlement, much medieval fortification, and, of course, our own times. You may well be struck by the very Neapolitan way the splendours of the past are found alongside the most mundane modern buildings. Or how graceful inner courtyards come to be strewn

with drying washing and cluttered with parked scooters. But as long as washing needs to dry, and scooters must be parked, that's how it will be, even if it means latter-day balconies are thoughtlessly allowed to disfigure once-graceful Baroque façades. It's all part of what happens when people continue to live right in the heart of a city. While Naples may not offer the best range of classic clothing, it does have its own talented designers, and is the birthplace of world-renowned accessories, such as Marinella ties, Valentino shoes and Tramontano handbags. Shoppers revel, too, in the quality and variety of its crafts. Bookbinders, fine leather goods craftsmen, glovers, goldsmiths, lute-makers and figurine artists are all still to be found working in the historic city centre, while coral craftsmen and jewellers work in Torre del Greco, Amalfi is the home of handmade paper, and Vietri is famous for its ceramics. Many interesting items can be found on roadside stalls, selling for only a few thousand lire. There's great variety, too, in Neapolitan

cuisine, which nowadays ranges from humble rustic dishes to the most sophisticated creations, so there's something to suit every budget. If you're fond of seafood you're in luck, since the city abounds in restaurants offering delicious dishes, with squid, octopus and swordfish available in many different guises. And once you've tasted a *margherita* pizza in Naples, you may find it harder to eat one anywhere else. You'll also discover the Neapolitan passion for coffee and taste enticing pastries with musical names, such as *babà*, *sfogliatella*, and *pastiera*. And even if you've come to see Pompeii or to enjoy the sunny charm of the Amalfi coast, you're sure to find you're drawn back to the play of light and shade in the *vicoli*, the sights and smells of the open-air markets, the taste of *taralli* bought from a street vendor, and the peculiar sound of your own footsteps on the worn black lava paving stones.

How to get there

Like all Mediterranean cities, Naples is a delight when the sun shines, but drab and dreary when it rains. The climate is mild, but in spring and autumn the weather can sometimes be wet and unpredictable – a sudden heavy shower can be followed by brilliant sunshine. The sea is warm enough for swimming until mid-November, so bring your swimming gear whatever the season. You may also want to time your visit to coincide with one of the city's popular festivals to see the Neapolitans in party mood.

WHEN TO GO

May and December are probably the best months. The 'Monuments in May' initiative was launched in 1994. Every weekend in May visitors can visit the city's monuments free (guided tours are available), and a number of major works of art are on view to the public during this period only.

Inevitably, it means there's an influx of visitors in the month of May.

December is the ideal time to see Naples at its most authentic, when Christmas preparations are under way. A variety of special pastries are prepared for the festive season, and the final touches are put to the miniature figurines that are an integral part of the famous Neapolitan crib scenes. But the days are short, and the weather, while never really cold, is often wet.

The best months for swimming in the sea are June and September, when the beaches aren't over-crowded –

TRADITIONS AND PROCESSIONS

On the feast of Sant'Antuono (Sant'Antonio Abate's Day), on 17 January, Christmas trees are traditionally burnt in some of the city's squares. This is a dying tradition that's both dangerous and illegal.
Make sure you attend the street procession in Procida on Good Friday (6 January) (see p.67).
The feast of the Madonna of the Arc is celebrated in the village of Sant'Anastasia on Easter Monday.
The festival of the Miracle of the Blood takes place on the first Saturday in May, and the procession for the feast of San Gennaro is on 19 September (see p.36).
Christmas festitivities are at their height on 8 December.
New Year's Eve in Naples is a unique event. Starting at midnight for a whole hour, the city is ablaze with fireworks.
The best vantage point is a balcony – set foot in the streets at your peril.

It's also the time of year when many festivals take place. If you find very hot weather unbearable, it's best to avoid July and August.

PUBLIC HOLIDAYS AND FESTIVALS

Christmas Day, Easter Sunday and Easter Monday (*Pasquetta*), Labour Day (1 May), 15 August (*Ferragosto*), and All Saints' Day (1 November) are all public holidays. There are other public holidays worth noting, especially as everything is closed: 25 April is Liberation Day, 19 September is the Festival of San Gennaro, Patron Saint of Naples, and 8 December is the Day of the Immaculate Conception. These last two are truly festive occasions (see yellow box).

HOW TO GET THERE

It's best to fly if you're only spending a weekend in Naples.

FROM THE UK

British Airways runs two daily services to Naples from London Gatwick irport, or you can go with Alitalia via Milan Malpensa or Rome Fiumicino airports. From Rome, you can take the Intercity train from the central railway station, Termini, on to Naples. There's a reliable shuttle service, leaving every 30 minutes, between Rome Fiuminicino and the station, and the train journey takes under two hours. Departures are hourly until 9.10pm.

FROM ELSEWHERE

There are no direct flights from the US, Canada, Australia or New Zealand to Naples.

CONTACTS

British Airways
General reservations
☎ 0345 222111 or BA Victoria Station office, 115 Buckingham Palace Rd SW1 9SJ ☎ 020 7707 4747.

Alitalia
4 Portman Square, London W1H 9PS
☎ 020 7486 8432.

you can't move on them in July and August – and the water temperature is heavenly, even in late summer.
The quality of the light in autumn is sublime, while everything begins to bloom in spring, especially on the islands.

Qantas or
Air New Zealand
Will ticket onward via their
European hubs, Frankfurt
or London. Some North
American airlines fly into
Milan or Rome and will
arrange onward connections
to Naples.

IN NAPLES

Alitalia's Naples office is
at Capodichino Airport
☎ 081 709 33 33, and is open
6am-9pm.

British Airways has no
office in Naples but their local
agent is G.E.S.A.C., who is
also at the airport.

INCLUSIVE BREAKS

Many tour operators offer
three or four-day weekend
breaks that include travel and
accommodation to suit all
tastes and pockets. Dates can
be pre-scheduled or you can
choose your own. These
breaks can be reasonably
priced and you can stay in a
luxury hotel at only a
moderate cost. For a list of
tour operators who offer
weekend breaks in
Naples, write to the
**Italian State
Tourist Office**,
1 Princes
Street,
London
W1R 8AY
☎ 020 7408
1254, or call
**Bridge
Travel
Services**,
55-59 High
Road,

Broxbourne, Herts EN10 7DT
☎ 01992 456 600, or
Magic Cities,
227 Shepherds Bush Road,
London W6 7AS
☎ 020 8563 8959
☏ 020 8748 3731.

CAR HIRE

If you only intend to visit
Naples, the islands and
Pompeii, you're strongly
advised not to use a car. There
are massive traffic jams, car
parks are rare, and Neapolitan
drivers are very creative, so
driving round the city can be
slow and stressful. In town,
it's far better to take metros,
buses and taxis, or to walk.
To get across the bay, take the
hydrofoils (*aliscafi*), or for
Pompeii, Herculaneum and
Cumae, take the *circum-
vesuviana* or the *cumana*
trains. If you plan a visit along
the Amalfi Coast or to the
Phlegraean Fields, try to avoid
Sundays or the high season,
when they're knee-deep in
tourists.

If you want the challenge of
driving, you can hire a car
through a tour operator or one
of the international car rental
companies before departure.
Reserving in advance will
always be cheaper than
renting locally on arrival. If
you do, you'll need to be over
21 and to have held a valid
driving licence for over a year.

ENTRY REQUIREMENTS AND CUSTOMS

Citizens of the European
Union must have a valid
identity card or passport.
Travellers from the USA,
Canada, Australia and New
Zealand require a valid
passport and are limited to a
90-day stay.

Italy is a signatory of the
Schengen agreement, so
European Union citizens no
longer have to pass through
customs on arrival in the
country. However, should you
have any doubt regarding
what you can bring into
Italy, contact your nearest
international airport.

FROM THE AIRPORT TO THE CITY CENTRE

Naples'
Capodichino
Airport is only
about 20
minutes from the
city centre. The 14
bus goes from the
airport to the
Piazza Garibaldi
central
railway

HEALTH AND INSURANCE

station. Remember to buy a ticket before you get on the bus, as tickets aren't sold on board. The best way of getting to the centre is to take a taxi, which is relatively inexpensive. The taxi stand is supervised, and the law requires prices (in both Italian and English) to be displayed inside the taxis. If prices are displayed on the back of the front seats, i.e. in plain view of passengers,

you've nothing to worry about. If, on the other hand, they're displayed alongside the driver, be more circumspect. There's a legitimate L5,000 supplement on all journeys from airport to centre or centre to airport and a L500 charge per item of luggage. There's also a L2,000 supplement on journeys made after 10pm at night, and L3,000 on public holidays.

No vaccinations are required prior to entering the country. The water in Naples, though high in calcium, is perfectly drinkable. If you're on a course of medical treatment, take enough medicines with you when you go, since you can't be sure of finding the same ones in Italy. If you fall ill, you may have to pay for your treatment, but you can be reimbursed. Before

departure, UK citizens should obtain an E111 form from the post office to claim a refund of any medical expenses incurred.

Make sure you have travel insurance that covers you adequately for loss of luggage and repatriation on medical grounds. Paying for your holiday or travel by credit card usually provides automatic insurance against loss of luggage or flight cancellations, but check with your bank for details. You can arrange travel insurance through your travel agent or insurance company.

LOCAL TIME

Italy is one hour ahead of Greenwich Mean Time. Summertime starts at the end of March, when clocks are put forward an hour, and wintertime at the end of September, when clocks go back an hour.

BUDGETING FOR THE TRIP

Naples is not only less expensive than cities like London or New York,

prices are also lower than in cities in central and northern Italy. Of course, your budget will depend on your tastes, but expect to spend around L500,000 for the weekend, not including accommodation, transport and souvenirs. As long as you don't eat in fancy restaurants and avoid tourist traps, a meal costs on average L25,000-30,000. A bus or metro ticket costs L1,500, a return trip to Capri by hydrofoil costs L34,000, entrance to museums or archaeological sites is L8,000-12,000 and a drink in a bar or nightclub L10,000-15,000 – so you see, nothing is very expensive in itself. How much you spend on souvenirs and presents is very much up to you – the choice is wide, with everything from lemon-flavoured liqueurs (L15,000) to Prada handbags.

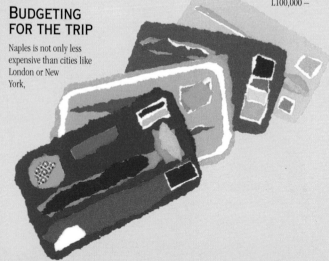

Italy is one of the European Union countries that joined the single currency, and from 2002 the Euro will replace the Lira. 1 Euro = L1936.27. In the meantime, all prices are listed in both Lire and Euros.

When changing money before departure, ask for some small-denomination banknotes – L10,000, L50,000 or L100,000 –

as larger notes are hard to change without incurring the wrath (and sometimes refusal) of shopkeepers and clerks.

DON'T TEMPT FATE

There are thieves and pickpockets in Naples as elsewhere. Avoid showing off expensive jewellery (or jewellery that just looks expensive). Keep money safe in deep pockets, preferably with buttons, or handbags with good, strong zips, and don't walk around with all your worldly wealth about you. Many hotels have safes where you can leave valuables, but make a photocopy of all your documents in case of loss. Taking such simple precautions should ensure you have a relaxed stay.

However, for emergency assistance if you do run into trouble – to replace a stolen passport or worse – contact your nearest consulate or embassy. Representative offices aren't open 24 hours a day, but there'll usually be a recorded message giving a number for use in emergencies. Help will be just a phone call away.

VOLTAGE

In Italy, the current is 220 volts. Italian plugs have two or three flat pins and you may need to use an adaptor. It's a good idea to bring one with you if you want to be sure of using your electric hair dryer or razor during your stay.

USEFUL ADDRESSES

IN THE UK

Italian State Tourist Board
1 Princes Street
London W1R 9AY
☎ 020 7408 1254
🖷 020 7493 6695

Italian Consulate
38 Eaton Place
London SW1
☎ 020 7235 9371

Italian Cultural Institute
39 Belgrave Square
London SW1
☎ 020 7235 1461
🖷 020 7235 4618

Italian Book Shop
8 Cecil Court
London WC2
☎ 020 7240 1634

CIT Italian Tourist agency
Marco Polo House
3-5 Lansdowne Rd
Croydon CR9 1LL
☎ 020 8686 5533
🖷 020 8681 0712
e-mail ciao@citalia.co.uk

IN NAPLES

British Consulate
Via Francesco Crispi, 122
☎ 081 66 35 11
🖷 081 76 37 20

Tourist Information
Piazza Plebiscito
(inside Palazzo Reale)
☎ 081 41 87 44
🖷 081 41 86 19

Police
☎ 113

UNDER THE VOLCANO

Mount Vesuvius is the emblem of Naples, and its familiar form dominates the bay. Revered by Neapolitans, the volcano is seen as a symbol of both destruction and fertility, and is the subject of many legends. Its anger is likened to that

of a god or devil that only San Gennaro can appease. And yet, despite the danger of fresh eruptions, people still clamour to live on the foothills of Vesuvius.

NOT ONE VOLCANO BUT TWO

The Vesuvius we know today first appeared in the 3rd century AD inside an older volcano called Mount Somma. Since then, its history has been one of long periods of dormancy interspersed with sudden awakenings. Its contours have been

A layer of ashes covers Naples following an eruption

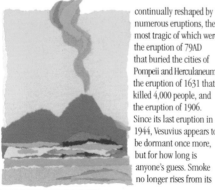

continually reshaped by numerous eruptions, the most tragic of which were the eruption of 79AD that buried the cities of Pompeii and Herculaneum, the eruption of 1631 that killed 4,000 people, and the eruption of 1906. Since its last eruption in 1944, Vesuvius appears to be dormant once more, but for how long is anyone's guess. Smoke no longer rises from its

crater as in the old photographs, but it still remains a latent threat. The Vesuvius Observatory, which was founded in 1845, constantly monitors the volcano's activity and eruptions can now be predicted a month in advance.

A LIVING, BREATHING LAND

Rising smoke, sulphurous vapours (*solfatare*), warm springs with supposedly medicinal properties and often undetectable tremors are all reminders of the constant activity below the ground of the Campania region, where the most recent earthquake of 1980 claimed the lives of over 1,500 people. The ground level in the volcanic area known as the Phlegraean Fields slowly rises and falls, and this semblance of 'breathing', termed bradyseism, has on numerous occasions led to the evacuation of the historic centre of Pozzuoli.

CHRIST'S TEARS

A local legend has it that, while travelling the world, Christ arrived one day in Campania. He climbed to the summit of Mount Vesuvius, whereupon he beheld the magnificent view and said, 'This is an earthly paradise, but its inhabitants are real devils'. The thought of this made him start to cry, and where his tears fell, women planted vines. Since then, these areas of volcanic soil have produced one of Italy's best wines, the Lachryma Christi (Christ's Tear), a white wine that should be drunk lightly chilled (10°C/60°F) in order to retain its flavour.

COVETED SLOPES

Since ancient times, people have been drawn by the lure of the volcano, despite the obvious danger. At present, 700,000 people live in this high-risk area, no doubt for many reasons – the fertile soil, the beautiful setting and the chronic shortage of living space in Naples itself. In fact, thousands of residential buildings have been built here without planning permission since the last eruption. However, it's hoped the Vesuvius National Park, established in 1991, will act as a barrier against any further unbridled property speculation.

FUNICULÌ, FUNICULÀ

What from a distance appears as a long white scar carved into the side of the volcano is in fact the route of the old funicular railway. Despite several attempts to re-establish it, the funicular hasn't run since it went out of service after the eruption of 1944.

Its opening in 1880 was celebrated in the now-classic Neapolitan song, *Funiculì Funiculà*. Nowadays, only a good pair of walking shoes and the payment of L5,000 at the last 'toll' will guarantee your ascent to the crater. There's a standard family route or a more demanding itinerary for the energetic (contact Naples WWF ☎ 081 560 10 04 for details). The crater measures 600m/1,970ft in diameter and is 200m/656ft deep. It may look less impressive than that of Mount Etna, but on a clear day the view of the entire Bay of Naples is breathtaking.

A CHOCOLATE VOLCANO

This is the chocolate Vesuvius created by the Gay Odin patisserie on the occasion of the G7 summit in Naples in 1994. Instead of lava, it has nutty chocolate wrapped in a layer of delicious dark chocolate, and a crater overflowing with nuts. It comes in its own presentation box in the chocolate-maker's colours (Prussian blue on a white background), and is available in four sizes costing from L5,000 to L70,000 for over 1kg/2lb of chocolate.

The 1906 eruption

THE CAMORRA

Though less well known than the Sicilian Mafia, the Camorra is far more than just a persistent local rumour. You're unlikely to witness the Camorra first-hand as a tourist – a street vendor selling contraband cigarettes is all you're likely to see – yet behind the scenes the organisation continues to blight the economic and social life of the city.

In a bid to fight crime, the authorities print the following warning on both telephone cards and billboards: 'Small misdemeanours lead to organised crime.'

TWO CENTURIES OF TROUBLE

The word *camorra* first appeared in the late 18th century, and was used to refer to a gambling club opposite the Royal Palace. It is thought *camorra* comes from *morra*, then a popular game of chance. Today the term refers to both an activity – extortion – and a seemingly indestructible criminal organisation. Despite periodic and apparently successful crackdowns, the Camorra always manages to rise from its ashes, especially as political and economic circumstances sometimes work in its favour.

NOT THE SAME AS THE MAFIA

The Camorra is made up of a hundred or so 'clans' and some 7,000 associates in the region. Gangs form and disband at an alarming rate and it is hard to be accurate regarding figures. The Camorra originated in the city, and controls both rich and poor parts of Naples. Its structure is less rigid than the Mafia's, and

young men can sometimes be bosses. At times, it recruits children (the so-called 'baby-killers') as messengers or small-time drug dealers. It's said to be responsible for around 250 deaths a year.

10,000 TONNES OF TOBACCO

This is the amount of tobacco smuggled into Italy each year in a variety of ways. In the past, the smugglers would paint their motor launches blue in order to avoid detection by coastguards. But contraband tobacco isn't all that interests them – the Camorra also runs many other rackets, including loan-sharking, extortion, prostitution, drug dealing, illegal lotteries and even arms trading. Part of the Camorra's power and influence is the

A break from duty at the police station

result of occasional collusion with dishonest politicians and the embezzlement of public funds.

AN UNORTHODOX TAXMAN

It was quite common for a visitor arriving in Naples by boat in the 1860s to see a stocky individual receiving several coins from the ship's captain as the passengers disembarked. This 'taxman' was usually better dressed than those around him, wore numerous rings and fancy jewellery and generally acted as if he were the boss. If a visitor enquired who this man was, he'd quietly be told it was a member of the Camorra. While there's thankfully no chance of coming across such a character on your travels nowadays, the racket still exists.

THE GUAPPO (PRONOUNCED '*WUPP*')

At the beginning of the 20th century, the small-time thug (who was often a camorrista), wore a check jacket, pale green shoes, and a hat cocked over one eye. Times may have changed, but his present-day counterpart still displays the same insolence and showy dress sense, and is often found wearing a hat and a lot of jewellery, especially on festive occasions.

SIGARETTE, SIGARETTE

In Naples you're never far from someone selling black market cigarettes. These vendors are generally tolerated by the authorities, and mostly looked on benevolently by Neapolitans, who describe themselves as *fumatori accaniti* ('chain-smokers').

ONE OF THE MYSTERIES OF NEAPOLITAN LIFE

As you stroll down a quiet alleyway, you may come across a crumpled old cigarette pack on the door of one of the *bassi* (houses). Knock on the door and an old woman will let you in, whatever time of day or night it is. Tell her your favourite brand of cigarettes and another old woman will reach into a large basket and pass you what you ordered. All that remains for you to do is pay. The women will then return to their knitting, and you'll be free to leave.

During your stay, you'll notice their wares laid out on makeshift stalls, and hear the rallying cry '*Sigarette, sigarette*' in bars and across café terraces everywhere. Prices vary according to mood, brand and demand, but the average price is L3,500–L4,500. In case you're at all tempted, bear in mind that most Neapolitans avoid Marlboros and Camels.

LEATHER GOODS, HAUTE COUTURE AND CRAFTSMANSHIP

Unlike most other large European cities, Naples still has many craft workshops in the very heart of the city. The production of leather goods grew out of the region's long-established tanning industry. The oldest parts of Naples each have their own particular speciality — gloves and shoes, for example, are made in Sanità, and fine leather goods come from Montesanto and the Spanish Quarter.

A LONG TRADITION

Naples is the Italian home of the leather glove. Glove-making first started in the 18th century, and expanded rapidly in the early years of the 19th. The presence of the Bourbon court in Naples helped to spread the popularity of an accessory already prized for its beauty and quality. However, its popularity began to wane in the 1970s, when a pair of gloves came to be considered simply a practical item, and world competition in the industry grew.

TRUE CRAFTSMANSHIP

The traditional method of making a pair of gloves involves at least 15 people, and is carried out from cut to finishing in 25 different stages. Most of these are done by hand, and are entrusted to women working from home in the Sanità quarter or in villages around Naples. Finding highly-skilled workers, cutters and stitchers is becoming increasingly difficult, not least because the average age of those working in this sector is very high, which means that the future of the Neapolitan glove is far from certain.

THE OMEGA, GLOVERS

The Omega workshop is housed on the third floor of a building in the heart of the Sanità quarter. Its owner, Mauro Squillace, one of the youngest entrepreneur-glovers in Naples, is always glad to explain the finer points of glove-making (handed down through three generations of his family) to visitors. Known for the quality of their leather, Omega gloves come in a wide choice of colours. The house speciality is the

classic-cut glove with a silk or cashmere lining. A visit will allow you to witness at close hand the meticulous attention paid to detail, a rarity in so many modern industries. (Via Stella, 12 ☎ 29 90 41, Mon.-Fri. (9am-1pm, 2-8pm).

CUT AND COMFORT

There are a number of factors to look out for when buying a pair of gloves. To see whether the leather has been cut correctly, pull the glove lengthwise – a well-cut glove should hardly give. Then pull it widthwise – this time it should give, as some stretch is needed to ensure that it will be comfortable. Make sure, too, that the gloves you buy are half-lined. For them to be comfortable, the silk lining should not be stuck directly onto the leather, but rather be a glove in itself that has been

inserted and attached at a later stage. For maximum warmth and comfort, the fingers of the glove should also be lined.

MARIO VALENTINO

Mario Valentino is the only large-scale manufacturer of shoes and fine leather goods in southern Italy. The company, which enjoys a worldwide reputation, is located right in the heart of the working-class Sanità district, near the Fontanelles cemetery. Backing onto a wall made of volcanic material, the Valentino factory is housed on three floors and employs over two hundred people, in stark contrast to other companies in the sector, which rarely employ more than ten.

HANDBAGS ON THE SLY

Handbags are the youngest branch of the leather trade.

THE GENUINE AND NOT-SO-GENUINE

Many craftsmen earned their living by making imitation designer bags until the designers in question (Versace, Vuitton, Chanel, Lancel and others) began to get worried, and with good reason –the imitation bags were made to a very high standard. Nowadays checks are more rigorous, and since the early 1990s fewer imitation bags have been produced, though you're bound to see a few on market stalls.

Their manufacture started long after that of gloves and shoes, and has never relied on people working from home. Production is mainly based in the working-class districts of the city, sometimes in tiny street-level workshops known as *bassi*. Even though they're sometimes involved in the manufacture of bags for top Italian and foreign designers, not all these small-scale craftsmen are known to the taxman.

THE BAROQUE

Naples is the archetypal Baroque city, where the flamboyance and lavishness of the architecture is echoed in the theatricality of daily life in the noisy streets. Much of the spirit of the Baroque has survived intact, and can be seen in the Neapolitans' way of taking each day as it comes, never forgetting the ephemeral nature of life, appreciating spur-of-the-moment pleasures, paying minute attention to appearances, and hiding faded interiors behind splendid façades. The streets will provide your first insight into the Neapolitan Baroque, an unruly architecture now four centuries old.

The Capella Sansevero

THE BAROQUE AND THE COUNTER-REFORMATION

Baroque religious fervour gripped the city in the late 16th and early 17th centuries. Spanish-controlled Naples, with its proximity to Rome, was fertile ground for the church during the Counter-Reformation. The inhabitants of the city quickly adopted the new modes of worship, and the change soon became apparent not only in people's attitudes but also in the make-up of Naples itself, as convents, lay brotherhoods, pilgrimages and miraculous images multiplied.

CATASTROPHES, AND PATRON SAINTS PATRONS

The deadly eruption of Vesuvius in 1631, the uprising

Bacchus by Caravaggio

led by Masaniello in 1647 and the plague epidemic of 1656, which killed half the city's 600,000 population, put fear in the hearts of the people. It also had a dramatic effect on the arts, the proximity of death leading to heightened religious feeling. During the Baroque era, saints, relics and miracles proliferated, and the people's need for supernatural protection became so urgent

that in the space of 120 years the number of intercessors the Neapolitans could call on to pray for them rose by 410!

CARAVAGGIO

The upheavals of the century are clearly reflected in the moody and dramatic style of Caravaggio's paintings. In *The Seven Acts of Mercy*, a painting in the Church of Pio Monte

Boy with a Club Foot by José de Ribera

A pinnacle of Baroque art can be seen in the spectacular monumental stairways of Ferdinando Sanfelice. It was Sanfelice who was first to set a stairway at the back of a courtyard and make it a decorative feature. In his hands, the stone stairway became a thing of great beauty, full of spaces, curves and arcades. His ornamental doorways and stairways make buildings airy and light even when they're in need of restoration. Some of the best examples of his work can be seen in the palaces of Sanfelice, Spagnolo, Serra di Cassano and Spinelli di Laurino (Via Tribunali, 362) and Mastellone (Largo Carità, 5).

della Misericordia (Via Tribunali, 253, Mon.-Sat. 9.30am-1.30pm), harsh contrasts of light and shade are used to depict the pathetic figures of the beggar, the old man in prison and the dead body seen by the light of the priest's candle. Despite the brevity of his stay in Naples, an artist of Caravaggio's stature was sure to influence local artists. Remarkable examples of the Neapolitan Baroque school – Spadaro, Ribera, Caracciolo, Vaccaro, Giordano and Solimena – can be seen in the church of the Certosa San Martino (Largo San Martino, see p. 48).

BAROQUE SUFFERING

The depiction of suffering that was so evident in paintings can also be found in works of

sculpture. Fanzago's works bear the stamp of the macabre. The skulls decorating the small cemetery disturb the quiet Renaissance setting of the main cloister of the Certosa San Martino, as do the skulls and leg bones to be seen on either side of the altar and on the exterior of the Church of Santa Maria delle Anime del Purgatorio (see p. 39).

THE SPLENDOUR AND MISERY OF THE BAROQUE AGE

Yet amidst this whirlwind of sentiment, the Baroque also had its quiet moments. Cloisters, often decorated with statues and tiles, can provide an oasis of calm and light set back from the labyrinth of dark side streets. The interiors

The Gesù Nuovo Church

of many churches are sumptuously decorated. Plump little *putti* (angels) smile mockingly down alongside the macabre grimaces of skeletons. The gold stuccowork interior of the Church of San Gregorio Armeno, the resplendent multi-coloured marble and onyx interior of the Gesù Nuovo Church and the lavish decoration inside the Capella Sansevero were all intended to be reassuring mirages, a respite from the rigours of daily life.

The Church of San Gregorio Armeno

FESTIVALS

In the past, performances and festivities were usually held in the piazzas, which were often adorned with fountains and sculpted marble spires (*guglie*). Three of the latter can still be seen in Naples – in the Piazza Gesù, Piazza San Domenico and Piazza Sisto Riario Sforza. The fountains were a protection against fire, and the large spires were designed to ward off eruptions and the outbreak of epidemics. They were part of the tradition of building temporary structures on festive occasions, which were intended to be burnt and which are still part of the *gigli* festivities in the village of Nola on the last Sunday in June.

PIZZA

Neapolitan pizza is the best in the world. Pizza has long been seen as a symbol of Naples and Neapolitan cuisine. Indeed, there are many Neapolitans who will tell you that life wouldn't be the same without it, and neither would meals with friends the world over. Pizza is a food meant for all the senses, and for all people. But remember, it's often pizzas with the simplest toppings that taste the best.

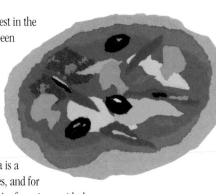

DISPUTED ORIGINS

Many towns lay claim to being the birthplace of pizza, and there's evidence to suggest that pizzas already existed in Italy as far back as 3,000 years ago. The word 'pizza' may be derived from the Latin *picea*, which was a piece of flattened dough cooked on a heated sheet of metal. Setting aside the disputed origins of pizza – even if it wasn't created in Naples, Naples certainly adopted it – it was here that they first acquired their reputation before going on to conquer the world.

DIVINE PIZZA

This simple, everyday means of sustenance is said to have divine origins. During the course of the long search for her daughter Persephone, the goddess Demeter one day saved the life of the son of her hosts, King Celeo and Queen Metarina. Later on, Metarina caught Demeter making the boy walk through fire to render him immortal. Demeter was so furious at being spied on that she only calmed down when

offered a mixture of flour, water and basil, cooked over a fire. Which would mean that pizzas don't only satisfy hunger, they also appease the fury of the gods!

SENSUAL PLEASURES

Eating pizza involves all the senses at once. The eyes are drawn by the contrasting colours of the ingredients, the ear by the crackling of the oven (which must be wood-fired). The sense of smell is tantalised by the mingling of the different aromas, and the taste-buds by the pizza's flavour. Lastly, the sense of touch comes into play as your fingers take hold of a slice of warm, flour-dusted pizza.

A HINT OF VIRILITY

The secret of a good pizza lies in the artful combination of simple ingredients – flour, water, yeast, salt, basil, oregano, garlic and oil. The cooking process brings together the basic elements of life – earth, water, air and fire.

But the magic ingredient is the skill of the *pizzaiolo* (pizza cook). Popular belief has it that cooking a pizza is a man's responsibility, as only a man can provide the essential masculine touch that allows the dough to rise.

THE HUNGER OF PULCINELLA AND THE GREED OF KINGS

In Naples, pizza is where aristocratic tastes meet popular tradition – everyone loves going for a pizza. It can satisfy the appetite of the poorest and the gluttony of Pulcinella (the stock comic representation of a Neapolitan), and is equally enjoyed by the rich and powerful. It's said that King Ferdinand II used to slip into the Pizzeria del Testa incognito in 1835 to enjoy a 'Neapolitan pancake' prepared by the legendary pizzaiolo Domenico.

MARGHERITA

In 1889, the *pizzaiolo* Raffaele Esposito was summoned to the Palazzo Capodimonte to prepare a pizza for the royal family. He made three different types, one of which (made with tomatoes, *mozzarella* and basil –

the Italian colours) pleased Queen Margherita so much it was named after her. The *margherita* pizza is still very popular in Naples, though other simple pizzas, such as the pizza *bianca*, with oil and cheese (*ricotta* or *rugola*) or the pizza *carrettiera* (with *friarelli* sausage), shouldn't be overlooked.

WHERE TO FIND REAL NEAPOLITAN PIZZA

The Vera Pizza Napoletana Association has produced a list of specifications that sets down all the basic rules for making true pizza. These include the use of *mozzarella* from a young female buffalo, San Marzano tomatoes and extra-virgin olive oil, which is easier to digest. All pizzerias that follow these guidelines display the white, green and red 'Vera pizza napoletana' sign. Of course, that's not to say a pizza can't be excellent elsewhere.

18TH-CENTURY NAPLES

The arrival of the Bourbons in the 18th century marked the elevation of Naples from colony to capital of the Kingdom of the Two Sicilies. All new building would reflect this change in status. The Baroque style adapted accordingly, while the discovery of Herculaneum and Pompeii brought Classicism back into fashion, and Naples' renown spread throughout Europe. However, the Age of Enlightenment, which opened with the ideas of Giambattista Vico and abounded with intellectual and artistic activity, ended in 1799 with the bloodshed of the failed Parthenopean revolution.

Giambattista Vico (1668-1744)

A HOSTEL FOR THE POOR

In the 18th century, civil works overtook religious architecture in importance, and were often entrusted to architects from Rome. In 1751 the king commissioned Ferdinando Fuga to build the Albergo dei poveri, a hostel for the poor.

The result was an austere, imposing edifice, measuring 354m/1,160ft in length. Today only the façade in Piazza Carlo III remains, as most of the building collapsed in the 1980 earthquake.

VERSAILLES IN CASERTA

The year 1751 was also the year King Carlo III commissioned the architect Vanvitelli to build the Reggia di Caserta almost 20 miles outside Naples. This Neapolitan Versailles was to become the new royal residence and attract European aristocracy to the court. It was part of an ambitious plan to redesign the city that was never completed. The palace and its immense grounds remain a model of order and symmetry,

Giovanni Battista Pergolesi (1710-1736)

but the Farnese collection of Classical statuary and the treasures from Pompeii have already found their way to the Museo Archeologico Nazionale.

MUSIC

The 18th century was the golden age of Neapolitan music. It reached its zenith in the dramatic style of Scarlatti and the popular *opera buffa*, a form of comic opera that had its roots in street theatre. The highly-acclaimed works of Pergolesi and Cimarossa imbued operas and operettas of the period with new life and rhythms. Both composers had their works performed at the San Carlo Theatre (inaugurated in 1737), and at courts throughout Europe.

ARGENIO

This shop in Via Filangieri describes itself as former purveyor to the Bourbon Royal House of the Two Sicilies. It's here that admirers of King Carlo III and his descendants will find silk scarves, brooches and cuff links (L80,000), all bearing the royal coat of arms.

THE MYSTERIOUS PRINCE OF SANSEVERO

The Capella Sansevero clearly shows the ambivalence of Prince Raimondo, a man torn between the modernity of the Enlightenment, the

Sculpture in the Capella Sansevero

ancient traditions of alchemy and Baroque manners. There's certainly something devilish about the two cadavers in the crypt that have been preserved with their blood systems intact. On the other hand, an entirely opposite and altogether more modern intention is evident in the statues of *Self-control* and *Sincerity* that decorate the Prince's own tomb (see p. 39).

THE PARTHENOPEAN REPUBLIC

The French Revolution and its idea of freeing the masses struck a chord in Neapolitan intellectual circles, and in 1799 the Parthenopean Republic was proclaimed under the protection of the French army. The move was never understood by the anti-French population of Naples, and the Republic lasted only six months before ending in bloodshed. The ringleaders were either hung or beheaded on Piazza Mercato, the traditional site of executions.

PALAZZO SERRA DI CASSANO

The main entrance to one of Naples' most imposing Baroque palaces was once at no. 67 Via Egiziaca Pizzofalcone, opposite the Palazzo Reale (Royal Palace). However, this doorway was closed by order of Prince Serra as a sign of mourning for his

DIALECT AND NEAPOLITAN UNITY

In the 18th century the enlightened spirits of the upper middle classes decided to use the Neapolitan dialect to spread their own ideas. The attempt proved futile, and their ideas remained far removed from popular culture. However, the lower middle classes followed their example in the 19th century and tried to win the support of the feared masses by taking over their language. The *canzonetta* (popular song) and *sceneggiatura* (popular melodramatic comedy) played an active role in creating a common language that promoted 'Neapolitanness' and a new social cohesion. Nowadays, everyone from judges to street vendors speaks Neapolitan (which also contains words derived from Spanish, French, Arabic and German).

son, who was executed for taking part in the Parthenopean Republic. On 25 April 1995, the national holiday, the mayor of Naples, Antonio Bassolino, had the entrance solemnly reopened for a day, perhaps to symbolise the return of justice to the city.

THE CULINARY CALENDAR

To visit Naples and not learn more about its culinary traditions would be to miss much of the spirit of the city. The year is marked by a cycle of religious festivals associated with culinary rituals, all with a hint of paganism. The seasons are signified by the changing colours and smells emanating from the delicious pastries. Orange blossom once marked Easter and the start of spring. Today, a quick glance in a patisserie window will let you know when it's arrived.

FEBRUARY

No sooner have the stalls for Epiphany (6 January) been put away and the bonfires for Sant'Antonio (17 January) died down, than the city comes to life again for the carnival. It's a chance for parents to dress up their children, but also the best time of year to enjoy all kinds of fritters (*fritelle*, *grafe*, and *chiacchiere*) and lasagne made with *ricotta* and *ragù*, now traditionally eaten on Shrove Tuesday.

MARCH

Two unmissable events take place on San Giuseppe (19 March). The first is the bird market in Via Medina, the second the appearance of fried or baked *zeppole* (doughnuts).

The latter is worse for the waistline, with traditional doughnuts topped with cherries and cream. In the past, this was also a chance for people to show off their new spring wardrobes.

EASTER

Easter is the best time of the year for both festive events and gastronomic specialities. On Maundy Thursday, the *struccio* (a tour of various churches that combines elements of the Christian and the pagan) ends with a mourning supper of *zuppa di cozze* (soup with mussels) or maruzze (sea snails). The well-known Madonna dell'Arco procession is held on Easter Monday (Pasquetta) and is a lively affair, with *battenti* (barefooted followers) running alongside flower-covered floats.

LIGHT SUMMER FOODS

The summer heats mean that people avoid gastronomic excesses and turn instead to ice creams, iced tea or coffee, *granite* and iced almond milk. Summer events include the celebrations (with firework displays) for the Madonna del Carmine (16 July in Naples) and Sant'Anna (26 July in Ischia), as well as midnight bathing to celebrate St John's Day, and a variety of concerts (such as the international festival of Ravello, and Sorrento musical evenings).

ALL SAINTS' DAY

Neapolitans often choose All Saints' Day (2 November) to visit the graves of loved ones. In the past, it was customary to follow this with a trip of a different kind to the inns beyond the old city walls, but this practice has now ceased. Other rituals, such as the buying of delicious *torroni dei morti* (nougat – hard or soft), are still observed.

CHRISTMAS FESTIVITIES

With Christmas celebrations officially commencing on 8 December (the Day of the Immacolata), Naples is already at its Christmas best long before 25 December. To mark the opening of the Christmas season, the mayor and the cardinal of Naples lay a wreath of flowers at the base of the ornamental spire in Piazza del Gesù, and the festive spirit soon spreads throughout the city. The Christmas

nativity scenes are set up early on, and it isn't long before all kinds of pastries appear in patisserie windows: *struffoli* (round fritters with honey and stewed fruits), *roccocò* and *cassatine*, all of which are Southern Italian specialities and very different

to the *panettone* found in Northern Italy. Christmas dinner on 24 December is traditionally based on fish – particularly *fritelle di bacalà* (cod fritters) and *capitone* (a kind of eel).

NEW YEAR'S EVE WITH A BANG

The week after Christmas sees a huge increase in the number of stalls selling firecrackers, as well as more harmless fireworks, such

as Bengal lights. New Year's Eve used to bring regular fatalities, so the number and size of bangers that can be bought has been limited for the past two years. Since then, no-one's been killed. The city traditionally holds its breath during the 'explosion' that lasts from 11pm to 1am, and it's customary to eat lentils and pigs' trotters as a symbol of prosperity in the coming year (as are *struffoli*).

NEAPOLITAN SPECIALITIES

Savoury dishes

Pasta e fagioli – pasta with white beans, sometimes served with mussels

Carne al ragù – meat with a sauce that's been simmered for a long time

Sartù di riso – one of the more sophisticated dishes

Patisserie

Babà (rum baba) – seen for its texture by some as a symbol of Naples well-known 'porosity', or openness to outside influences

Sfogliatelle (millefeuilles) – a pastry that originated in the Arab world, with shortcrust (*frolla*) or flaky (*sfoglia*) pastry filled with *ricotta*

Delizie al limone – profiteroles or sponge cake with lemon filling (for where to buy, see list of patisseries at back of guide).

Piazzas, *VICOLI* AND *BASSI*

The labyrinths of *vicoli* (narrow alleyways) in the heart of Naples lead onto bright, airy piazzas. Many house famous monuments, yet the centre is by no means an open-air museum, thanks largely to the Neapolitans who continue to live and work here in their natural, undisciplined way. The centre is a densely populated, lively place best appreciated in the course of a meandering stroll. And at night the dim lighting lends the streets a mysterious charm.

THE SATURDAY EVENING GET-TOGETHER

On weekends and summer evenings, the largest piazzas in Naples become the preserve of young Neapolitans. Expect to see them in the usual places – Piazza Amedeo, Piazza dei Martiri and Piazza San Nazzaro, a smart district in Naples, or Piazza del Gesù and Piazza San Domenico Maggiore in the historic city centre. Nothing in particular

happens – people chat, walk about, flirt, joke and drive around on scooters until late into the night.

PALLONETTI

When you come across a group of Neapolitan youngsters kicking a ball around in alleyways or small piazzas, remember they're simply carrying on a thousand-year-old tradition. *Pallonetti* was the name given during the Middle Ages to the

streets where all manner of ball games were played ('pallone' meaning 'ball'). The name lives on in Pallonetto di Santa Chiara and

Pallonetto di San Liborio, though most famous of all is

the Pallonetto di Santa Lucia, which has given its name to the surrounding area.

THE ART OF DAILY LIFE

Everyone is familiar with the image of washing hanging over the street in messy, multicoloured lines. However, fewer people are aware of an equally necessary feature of daily life, the bright-blue plastic baskets. These are attached to strings dangling from windows, and this common and ingenious pulley system is used to transport shopping, post and any other small items up to people living in old buildings without lifts.

THE RHYTHM OF LIFE

Life and death aren't just private matters in many parts of Naples, and are often announced in code. Whenever there's a birth in a residential building, a small blue ribbon (for a boy) or red ribbon (for a girl) is proudly displayed above the

doorway. Death notices, pasted up on walls, are still a common sight in the centre of Naples. Joys and sorrows are shared throughout the neighbourhood.

POPULAR RELIGION

Every alleyway seems to have its own altar, and no two are ever quite the same. Some are modest and half-forgotten, others showy and decorated with flowers, yet all continue to testify to the strong presence of religion in daily life. Below portraits of the Virgin Mary or a saint, you often see small figurines depicting sinners burning in the flames of hell. Some Neapolitans cross themselves whenever they pass by one of these small altars.

AT THE BARBER'S

Much of the colourful life of the *vicoli* is due to the continued presence of many small shops and craft workshops. Among the small, noble trades that have resisted the winds of change is the barber, who, for L5,000 offers you the forgotten delights of a comfortable leather chair, creamy fragrant mousse and the caress of an old-fashioned razor. Just sit back and relax, and listen to the buzz of conversation, ranging from the latest football results, to political debates, or maybe even the matrimonial plans of the eldest son – all in rapid Neapolitan.

BASSI

These street-level living quarters consist of a single room, which includes bathroom facilities. Once little more than dark caverns, with the front door the only source of natural light, most have now been modernised. Windows have been put in, revealing brand-new kitchens and giant-screen televisions, while scooters are parked inside at night. Though the *basso* is partly a reflection of the Neapolitan housing market, it's also part of a lifestyle to which many inhabitants of the city remain deeply attached.

MOZZARELLA AND *TAZZULELLA*

The names of these two great local specialities, whose popularity has long since spread throughout Italy, roll pleasurably off the tongue. *Mozzarella* is as white as a Neapolitan *caffè* is black beneath the foam. Considered a minor miracle, good coffee is an essential part of daily life – a sign of hospitality and a chance to take a break. It's no exaggeration to say that, in Naples, drinking coffee is fast becoming a ritual, complete with its own ceremony.

NA TAZZULELLA E CAFFÈ

In Neapolitan dialect, *na tazzulella e caffè* means a small cup of coffee. This cup of coffee is so much a part of everyday life that the Neapolitan singer Pino Daniele celebrated it in one of his songs. It's so strong it's drunk only in very small amounts. Neapolitans drink it throughout the day – from a quick sip in the morning to a cup standing at the bar after lunch or even late at night. For many, it's inextricably linked with having a cigarette, so much so that bus conductors, who until recently were responsible for making sure no-one smoked, actually let people holding cigarettes onto the bus if they say the magic words *ho appena preso il caffè* ('I've just had a coffee').

COFFEE OF EVERY KIND

Apart from the well-known strong black variety, coffee can be drunk in a variety of ways. With milk it becomes *cappuccino*. With only a drop of milk it's *macchiato*. If you need a pick-me-up, ask for *corretto* ('corrected'!), a coffee with a measure of liqueur. The *brasiliano* is for those of you with a sweet tooth, and comes with foamy milk sprinkled with chocolate powder. In summer people often ask for a *freddo* (iced coffee). As you can see, there's a coffee for all occasions. Remember, though, that coffee is often served with sugar (partly so the froth stays on the surface). If that's not to your taste or waistline, ask for an *amaro*.

THE SECRETS OF GOOD COFFEE

Of course, coffee is also prepared at home, where it's equally delicious, though not as strong as espresso. However, certain conditions must be met. Only a blend (*miscela*) of robusta and arabica coffee beans should be used, and it should be well roasted and finely (but not too finely) ground. The type of coffeepot is also important, as a real *machinetta napoletana* makes coffee by percolation, and not steam pressure, as in the case of espresso. The coffeepot should also not be too new. Lastly, the water plays a vital role – many Neapolitans will tell you that only water from Naples can guarantee truly excellent coffee.

trams would even make a ten-minute stop to allow passengers to watch the show. Only the Caflisch and the Gambrinus remain from the old days. However, many of the newer cafés that have appeared on the piazzas of the old city seem to want to revive the tradition.

HISTORICAL CAFÉS

The café has long played an important role in Neapolitan socialising. The fashion for elegant cafés reached its peak in the 19th century. By 1850, there were as many as 30 cafés on Via Toledo alone! Such cafés were meeting-places for writers and artists, as well as layabouts. Goethe and Verdi were regulars at the Gambrinus. Farces and other shows were also staged in cafés. The famous comic Mongelluzzo used to perform in front of the Turco. His talent was such that some

MOZZARELLA AND *FIOR DI LATTE*

Real mozzarella is *di bufala* ('from buffalo milk'). Immediately recognisable by its colour, which should be

snow-white, it differs from *Fior di latte*, made with cow's milk, that has a yellowish tinge. When cut, real *mozzarella* squirts milk, whereas *Fior di latte* merely oozes it. It's firm and consistent to taste, and never melts in the mouth. Sold in various forms, either as the usual small balls (*bocconcini*) or threaded (*treccia*), it should be conserved in its own milk, and never in a refrigerator, which would cause it to dry out.

MAKING *MOZZARELLA*

Buffalo milk is pasteurised at 120°C/248°F, which causes it to separate into three layers, only two of which will be used. The middle layer, or whey (*siero*), is used to make *ricotta* or butter, while the lower layer hardens and forms into blocks that are then cut into small pieces and sprinkled with boiling water to soften them and create a pasty substance, that can be formed into *mozzarella* balls.

DAILY LIFE IN POMPEII

'Though my heart trembles at the very memory ...' – so begins the second letter of Pliny the Younger in which he recounts the last day of Pompeii. However, the archaeological site itself, rediscovered in 1748, reveals more than any book could about the city that was stilled in August AD 79. Roman Pompeii is so well preserved that it's much more than an open-air museum, and the visitor strolling through its streets can easily imagine the orators in their togas, and the cries of the tradespeople in the market that made up the daily life of the city.

THE *DOMUS POMPEIANA*

Two influences can be seen in the architecture of the average Pompeiian town house – Roman (the *atrium*) and Hellenic (the peristyle). The atrium was an inner courtyard with an opening (*compluvium*) in the roof to allow rainwater to fall into a basin (*impluvium*) where it was collected. It was used to receive important clients and official visitors, while the peristyle was a kind of pleasure garden surrounded by porticoes opening into bedrooms and reception rooms.

A HEALTHY MIND...

While the children of aristocratic families were entrusted to nursemaids and Greek tutors for their education, those of poorer members of society could attend communal lessons conducted outdoors (under the portico in the forum, or on the exercise ground). However, as there was no obligation to attend school, many Pompeiians never learnt to read or write, and in later life would have to make use of public scribes. Another source of culture was the 'Large Theatre' and adjacent 'Small Theatre'. Performances were usually either comedies or tragedies, though other genres also existed, such as mime or *atellane* – a kind of popular farce that was perhaps the forerunner of the Commedia dell'arte.

...IN A HEALTHY BODY

Sport was very popular, and physical education played an important part in the daily life of the Romans. The *palestre*

was an exercise ground where men could practise weightlifting, wrestling and discus throwing. However, the large rectangular space was also used for slave markets and cock fights. For Romans, sport was little more than an excuse to prepare the body to better appreciate the bath taken afterwards in the *thermae* (bathhouses). There were three such establishments in Pompeii, all at the crossroads of major streets, a clear sign of their popularity.

GLADIATORS AND BEASTS

Pompeiians loved the games in the amphitheatre, where the gladiators were the main attractions.

Some gladiators were so popular they were known by name and hailed both in the ring and on the street, and even their love lives were common knowledge. However, combats were also staged between men and beasts, wild and domestic animals, and lions and gazelles – the whole programme designed to satisfy the most basic and bloodthirsty instincts of the crowd.

POMPEIIAN DEITIES

Everywhere present, religion was an integral part of daily life, and Pompeiians paid hommage to literally hundreds of gods. All seemed to coexist in harmony, as is indicated by the many remaining temples and statues to Roman gods (Jupiter, Juno and Minerva), Egyptian gods (Isis, Serapis and Anubis) and the gods of the city (Hercules, Bacchus

and Venus). But the greatest devotion of all was reserved for an earthly god – the Emperor.

SALVE LUCRUM : LONG LIVE PROFIT!

This phrase, found inscribed on a wall in Pompeii, shows that money matters played an important role. Much of the city's wealth was due to its geographic position. Pompeii was a port with links to the rest of the mainland, to Numidia (modern-day Algeria) and even to Asia. Its thriving economy also derived from the region's fertile soil. Agriculture was therefore the most important activity, and it was its success that allowed such advanced forms of commerce and craftsmanship to develop. Produce was sold in *tabernae*. Examples of these – bakers, jewellers, shoemakers, ironmongers, and shops selling clothes and wine – can be still be seen today all along the Via dell'Abbondanza.

THE LOTTERY, AND OTHER PASSIONS

At first sight, the Neapolitans' passion for football and the lottery seems so theatrical and exaggerated it might be thought ridiculous. However, both offer them the opportunity to realise their dreams. It's hardly surprising, then, that in a city where superstition is rife, every important event is turned into a number and made the object of a bet.

THE LOTTERY DRAW

A full-blown ceremony for the lottery draw takes place every Saturday evening at 8pm outside 17 (ironically the unlucky number in Italy!) Via del Grande Archivio, on the corner of Via San Biagio dei Librai. As three sets of precautions are always better than two, the weekly ritual takes place under the official supervision of a policeman and a lawyer, as well as the watchful gaze of a large crowd, and it's usually a blindfolded child who draws the numbers.

A FAMILY GAME

Though the lottery is a serious business in Naples, it's still a game, and a good opportunity for some family fun. It's traditional to play the lottery on Christmas and New Year's Day, and during the end-of-year festivities, (especially around San Gregorio Armeno), you'll find all kinds of small items relating to the lottery. These include boards with symbols written in both Italian and Neapolitan and wicker baskets from which to draw the lottery numbers (L10,000).

THE SMORFIA

Though *smorfia* in Italian means grimace, in Naples it's also the name of a board designed to help you interpret your dreams. Every dream corresponds to one of the 90 numbers on the board, and you need never pick your lottery numbers at random again. So if you dreamt about a dead man with a suitcase talking to a sewer rat last night, you need to play 48 – 58 – 5 – 89! There are many handbooks available to help you pick the right numbers, though some of them have different meanings, i.e. the number 19 represents both St Gennaro and laughter.

THE *CIUCCIO*, THE CLUB SYMBOL

The first *Seria A* league championships (equivalent to the UK's Premier League) were held in 1926-7, and proved a disaster for Naples football club. It lost every single match, only scored a point thanks to a draw, and came bottom of the league. The club became the laughing stock of the nation, and the Neapolitans self-mockingly decided that the city's horse emblem would be a more fitting symbol of the club if it were turned into a donkey (*ciuccio* in Neapolitan dialect). The satirical cartoons tracing the club's history are on display in the Cucciolo Bohemien restaurant (see p. 76), and are well worth seeing.

LO SCUDETTO

While the 1926-1927 season may have been an all-time low, the 1986-1987 was an apotheosis. After a 60-year wait, Naples football club, led by Maradona, won the *scudetto* (the Italian league trophy) for the first time. Pandemonium broke out, people danced in the streets, and the city was

literally painted blue and white, the team colours. That evening, long funeral processions were staged, and mock-up coffins of their opponents were paraded through the city.

BORGHETTI COFFEE

On days when football matches are being played, you'll almost certainly hear street vendors calling 'caffè Borghetti' at the tops of their voices around the stadium. This comes in a small recipient with a characteristic yellow lid, and its price varies according to the importance of the match (L1,500 or more). It conveniently allows fans attending the game to have coffee at half-time, though it's actually a coffee liqueur.

STADIO SAN PAOLO

The San Paolo stadium is located in Fuorigrotta, opposite the Campi Flegrei metro station. The stadium was inaugurated in 1971, and has an 80,000 capacity. The pitch is surrounded by an enormous ditch designed to ward off over-enthusiasm on the part of the fans. The team plays every second Sunday at 4pm, and it's a good idea to buy a seat in Curva B (the cheapest seats), which is where all the Naples supporters are. Tickets start from L25,000, and are always available at the last minute on the black market.

Naples
Practicalities

Qui Napoli

The magazine *Qui Napoli* should be your constant companion and 'bible'. It's published monthly and provides all manner of useful information (in both English and Italian) about cultural events, opening times of museums and monuments, major airline schedules, train and boat timetables, etc. It's free, and available from tourist information offices including the ones in the Palazzo Reale, Piazza Plebiscito and Piazza del Gesù.

GETTING AROUND NAPLES

Walking and public transport are the best ways of getting around Naples. Use a car only for trips outside the city. Buses, while useful, only skirt the historic city centre. There are few pedestrian streets (the lower section of Via Toledo, Via Chiaia and a part of Spaccanapoli), though on Sunday mornings some thoroughfares (Via Partenope, for example) are closed to traffic. Otherwise, you take your chances on foot along the narrow streets of the centre, ducking and diving to avoid cars and scooters.

METRO AND FUNICULAR

Naples has two metro lines. The Metropolicana FS, the more central, is run by Ferrovie dello Stato and serves the main areas. It travels east to west from the central railway station to Pozzuoli. Metros run 5.30am-10.20pm, at approximately 8-minute intervals, but because trains run on the same tracks, there are often delays. The second metro line, Metropolitana Collinare, links the suburbs to the north with the Vomero district. There are four funicular routes that get you relatively quickly between the centre and upper Naples. The Central (from Piazzetta Augusteo), Montesanto and Chiaia (by Piazza Amedeo) funiculars all go to the Vomero district, while the Mergellina funicular goes from Mergellina to Via Manzoni (in Posillipo). Funiculars run 7am-10pm, and are rapid and reliable.

BUSES AND TRAMS

Time was when to travel by bus in Naples was to take your life into your own hands – or so it seemed. Things have got better in recent years. If you want to visit outlying areas of the city by bus, it's often hard to find which bus lines you need, as they're poorly indicated, though there's now a map of bus routes that's available free from the tourist office in Piazza del Gesù. Buses are often packed in the rush hour. The new routes R1, R2, R3 and R4, and the circle routes (indicated by the letter 'C') run the most frequently. Although it has eased, the city's traffic is still chaotic and there's often gridlock.

TICKETS AND THE *GIRANAPOLI*

Remember to buy a ticket before you get on a bus – they're never sold on board. You can get them from tobacconists' and newsstands and in metro and funicular stations. Tickets need to be punched in the machines (or validated by hand) at the start of your trip. The Giranapoli system was started in 1995, and allows you to travel on the bus, tram, funicular and metro networks. A L1,500 ticket is valid for 90 minutes' travel, though this can only include one metro or funicular journey. A day ticket costs L4,500 (ANM agency, Via G. Marino, 1 ☎ 081 763 11 11).

TAXIS

It isn't expensive to take a taxi in Naples. For official taxis, a list of tariffs has to be displayed in the back of the cab so as to be most clearly legible to the passenger. Drivers displaying their tariffs in the front of the taxi tend to be more creative with their prices. Pay only the correct amount but be aware that there are legal supplements: pick-up charge L4,000, bank holiay supplement L2,000, night charge (10pm-7am) L3,000, L500 per item of luggage, L5,000 for an airport trip and L1,200 toll on the motorway leaving Naples. If you're worried about not finding a taxi at a station or in the street, call a radio taxi, which will cost you only L1,500 more.

Cotana
☎ 081 570 70 70

Napoli
☎ 081 556 44 44

Partenope
☎ 081 556 02 02

OUTSIDE NAPLES

BY CAR

It's worth sticking to two simple rules if you're driving. First, map out your route before you set off, as street signs aren't always clear. Secondly, avoid leaving or entering the city on Friday or Saturday evenings, or rushing off to the Amalfi or Sorrento coasts on a Sunday if you want to get there in the day. Traffic swarms out of Naples at weekends.

Consortaxi offers a range of excursions by taxi to places of interest outside Naples. Return fares vary between L80,000 and L200,000. Consortaxi, Calata San Marco, 24 ☎ 081 551 30 61, do a reasonably-priced round trip to Pompeii for L140,000, but time is limited to 2 hours. Tailor-made trips can be quoted separately, or information and other details can be found in *Qui Napoli*.

LOCAL TRAINS

Two services link the area to the north-west of Naples (leaving from the Montesanto railway station) and four cover the area to the south (leaving from Piazza Garibaldi, the entrance is at underground level). If you intend to visit the

small towns of the Phlegraean Fields, take the Cumana. For towns in the same direction but further inland, take the Circumflegrea. Trains run every 10 or 20 minutes, though only six trains a day stop at Cumes or Lake Fusaro. Trains run approximately 5.20am-9.45pm.

The Circumvesuviana, from Piazza Garibaldi, runs through the small towns of Vesuvius along the coast, connecting Herculaneum, Pompeii and Sorrento). There are four different services and, despite its name, the *accelerato* is the slowest. It's best to take a *diretto* or a *direttissimo*, though first make sure they're stopping at your destination. Trains run 4am-midnight, but avoid travelling very late at night.

BY COACH

Coach companies offer journeys in and out of Naples from outlying towns. While comfort can vary, coaches are particularly worth considering for visits along the Amalfi coast where there's no train service. Timetable, departure and arrival details are given in *Qui Napoli*.

BY BOAT

The islands in the bay can be reached either by ferry (*traghetto*) or by hydrofoil (*aliscafo*), as can the coastal towns of Sorrento and Positano. The hydrofoil is quicker (45 mins to Capri, instead of 75 mins), and departures are more frequent, taking the various companies offering this route as a whole. The ferry costs half as much and offers more on-deck seating, so you can admire the view and enjoy the sunshine.

Both ferries and hydrofoils depart from the Molo Beverello, right in the centre of Naples, by the Piazza Municipio. Hydrofoils only leave from the port in Mergellina, while ferries for Ischia and Procida leave from the port in Pozzuoli.

All timetable information is published in *Qui Napoli*. Caremar offers the best value for money. Sunday morning crossings from June to September are always packed, so it's best to book.

CAMPANIA TOURIST CARD

This card is particularly useful for a short stay. It costs L30,000 and entitles you to use all modes of public transport for up to 48 hours and provides 7-day insurance cover against theft and accident. It also gives you reductions on museum admission, and in cafés and restaurants displaying the Tourist Card logo.

It can be purchased at the airport, in most railway stations and in some hotels and travel agencies. Once the card has been validated, all you need to do is show it on request. It comes with instructions on how and where to use it.

GOING OUT INCOGNITO

Tourists can be targets for pickpockets and muggers, so if you really need to try out the latest Nikon or that video camera you've just bought, carry it in a strong bag with a strap that you can sling across your body, and avoid having it constantly on display. Try not to look too much like a tourist.

FINDING YOUR WAY

Just to confuse you, Via Toledo is normally called by its old name, Via Roma, and Neapolitans usually refer to the Corso Umberto as the Rettifilo. Street numbering is, to say the least, creative, and the logic is impenetrable, so always keep an eye on the numbers on the other side of the road.

MAKING A PHONE CALL

The Italians are telephone junkies. There are many orange public telephones around, though the mobile phone is the Italians' favourite gadget.

Public telephones aren't ideal for private conversations as there's often no cabin as such. Many now only accept phone cards (L5,000, L10,000 or L15,000), which you buy from tobacconists' (look for the sign of a black 'T' on a white background). Remember to break off the top left-hand corner before inserting the card into the slot. The only public telephones that still take coins are usually those inside cafés. Otherwise, there's the post office (PTP), though they close at 1.30pm.

To telephone abroad, dial 00 followed by the country code, then the number you require. Local numbers in Italy have to be dialled as if you were calling from outside the town or city. This means that all phone numbers in Naples should be preceded by 081 – as they are in the guide – unless another code is given in the case of more distant towns, such as Salerno.

When calling Naples from abroad, the country code for Italy is 39, followed by 081 and the number in Naples.

SENDING A LETTER OR POSTCARD

Stamps can be bought from tobacconists', but they quite often run out. Post offices are more reliable but they close at 1.30pm. Only the one in Piazza Matteoti is open in the afternoons (until 6pm).

To send postcards to European Union countries costs the same as a first-class stamp. In an emergency, ask at reception in your hotel. They'll usually have stamps.

CHANGING MONEY

Banks open 8.30am-1.30pm and 2.45-3.45pm Monday to Friday. To be sure of avoiding long queues, it's far better to change money before you arrive in Naples. If you need to get money, you'll get the best exchange rate using a bank cash machine in the city centre that accepts internationally-recognised credit cards. There are some automatic exchange machines, but these are few and far between and the exchange rates are likely to be unattractive.

GUIDED TOURS

There's no shortage of companies offering guided tours. Some organisations, for example Napoli Sotterranea, (☎ 081 44 98 21), specialise in visits to what lies beneath the modern-day city. If you want to visit the Fontanelle cemetery before it's officially reopened to the public, contact L.A.E.S. (Libera Associazione Escursionisti Sottosuolo ☎ 081 400 256).

For other options and ideas, look in the 'Guided Visits' section of *Qui Napoli*. You're sure to find something that appeals.

TIMETABLES

Naples has become more user-friendly for the tourist in recent years. Nevertheless, opening hours to different places of interest vary widely according to season. While the information in this guide has been checked, details can change, so it's wise to double-check by consulting *Qui Napoli* or telephoning direct. For details of 'monuments taking part in the 'Monuments in May' scheme, see the guides published by the city council listing what's open. These are on sale at newsstands.

PLANNING YOUR WEEKEND

To make the most of your time in Naples, it's a good idea to contact the Italian tourist office in your home country to plan some of your activities in advance.

UK ☎ 020 7404 1254
USA ☎ 212 245 4822 (NY)
☎ 310 822 0098 (LA)
☎ 312 644 0990 (Chicago)
Canada ☎ 514 866 7667
Australia ☎ 02 9247 1308

Around the Duomo

The area behind the Duomo, or cathedral, is a lesser-known part of Naples, often only seen on the way to the station. One reason why people don't go there is that it's known to be under the strict control of the Camorra (see pp. 12-13). Yet the area is safe, its narrow streets are lively and charming and the small markets are full of items that will take your fancy.

❶ The Duomo★★★
Via del Duomo
☎ 081 44 90 97
Mon.-Sat. 7.30am-12.30pm,
4.30-7.30pm, Sun. 5-7.30pm
Treasure of S. Gen. 8am-noon.

The cathedral is built on the site of a 5th-century pre-Christian basilica. Work on it first began in the 13th century, and the cathedral has since undergone significant alterations. The relics of Saint Gennaro have been housed in the Cappella del Tesoro (Treasure Chapel) since the 17th century. The chapel itself is a Baroque masterpiece built to thank San Gennaro for the end of the 1656 plague epidemic. The cathedral is worth a visit for the superb 4th and 5th-century mosaics in the baptistery alone.

❷ The brides of the Via del Duomo★
The Via del Duomo is a dream come true for brides-to-be, with window upon window of bewitching lace, organdie and satin swathed in clouds of tulle. The wedding dresses here are showy, made-to-measure and expensive, especially at

❸ THE MIRACLE OF THE BLOOD★★★

Every first Saturday in May and on 19 September, the Blood of San Gennaro, the city's patron saint, liquefies in the two phials in which it's kept in the cathedral. The ritual dates back to the 14th century, and is said to be prophetic – if the miracle is slow to take place or doesn't happen at all, great misfortune will befall the city. In accordance with tradition, the so-called 'relatives' of the saint (mostly old Neapolitan women) encourage the miracle to work by shouting exhortations and even insults. The processions from the cathedral to the Santa Chiara cloister are well worth seeing.

one of the best-known establishments, Ciancia, at no. 176. The cost of the dress is traditionally borne by the mother of the bride.

❹ Church of Santa Maria Donnaregina Vecchia★★★
Vico Donnaregina, 25
☎ 081 29 91 01
Sat. 9am-12.30pm
Entry free.

This church is a jewel of Gothic art with a long history. It had to be entirely rebuilt after earthquakes in 1293 and 1307 and has a single nave divided into two levels to create a separate area for the nuns. Make sure you see the tomb of Marie of Hungary in the crypt, and the Loffredo

Chapel with frescoes inspired by the works of Giotto. Their brownish tinge is the result of a fire in 1390.

❺ Antica Osteria Pisano★★★
Piazzetta Crocelle ai Mannesi
☎ 081 554 83 25
Mon.-Sat. noon-11pm.

Close to the cathedral, this small family restaurant efficiently run by Concetta offers excellent cuisine and a menu that changes daily according to what's on sale at the market. The pasta with *genovese* sauce, *scialatelli* (fresh green pasta with basil and seafood sauce) and *tiramisù* are really quite irresistible (expect to pay L20,000-25,000).

❻ Santa Maria della Pace hospital★★
Via Tribunali, 226
☎ 081 44 47 00/
081 45 85 39
Mon.-Sat. 9am-1pm
Entry free (charge during exhibitions).

The 80m/262ft-long Lazaretto gallery on the first floor of the palace, whose walls and ceilings are decorated with superb frescoes by G. Diano, was used to house lepers and later the infirm until the 1960s. Relatives and friends could come and see their loved ones from the inner galleries to avoid contagion. The hall was recently opened to the public and sometimes houses temporary exhibitions.

❼ Porta Capuana market★★
Mon.-Sat. 9am-2pm.

One of Naples' largest markets is held in Via S.

Antonio Abate, behind Porta Capuana. It sells fruit, vegetables, meat, poultry and cheese at unbeatable prices, along with household items, and is well worth a visit. The busiest time is Saturday mornings. Whatever you do, make sure you don't miss it.

Via Tribunali

The streets of Naples may look like a free-for-all, but in fact they're usually being shared harmoniously by pedestrians, scooters and children playing football. The streets off Via Tribunali are no exception, and offer a mosaic of working-class Naples, with roving tomato vendors selling pictures of the Virgin Mary alongside vegetables, humble food stores, Gothic and Baroque churches, pizzerias and street altars.

❶ Church of San Gregorio Armeno★★
Via San Gregorio, 44
☎ 081 552 01 86
Mon.-Fri. 9am-noon, Sat.-Sun. and holidays 9am-1pm.

Though originally built in the 8th century to house the relics of St Gregory, Bishop of Armenia, the convent was later divided into two parts to distance the nuns from the rest of the faithful. The church as it now stands dates back to the late 17th century and is decorated in an exuberant Baroque style, with sumptuous inlaid and gilt decorative woodwork and coffered wooden ceilings. The cloister is a charming mix of the sound of church bells, the discreet footfall of the nuns and Neapolitan cooking smells.

❷ Via San Gregorio★★
December 8 is the day of the *Immacolata*, and from November onwards the pretty Via San Gregorio has a festive feel. When the big day finally arrives, the street is lined with Neapolitan crib scenes with traditional nativity figures (a 400-year-old tradition), as well as more modern characters drawn from the worlds of showbiz, sport and politics. You'll need about two hours (as opposed to the usual five minutes) to make your way from one end of the street to the other.

❸ San Lorenzo★★★
Piazza S. Gaetano
☎ 081 29 05 80
☎ 081 45 49 48
Every day 7am-noon, 5-7.30pm. Arch. site every day exc. Tue. 9am-1pm, 4-6.30pm, Sun. 9am-1.30pm (entry charge).

This church commissioned by Charles I in the late 13th century is a jewel of Angevin Gothic art. It has a single nave leading up to the high altar by Da Nola, delicately set off by the ambulatory and nine radiating chapels. The tomb of Catherine of Austria by Tino di Camaino is quite wonderful. From the cloister you can descend below the church, from where you'll be able to see some of its history – over the Greek foundations are a Roman road and the remains of a pre-Christian basilica.

❹ The city below the city★
Piazza San Gaetano, 68
☎ 081 29 69 44
Mon.-Fri. guided tours at noon and 2pm, Sat.-Sun. 10am and 9pm, Thu. 9pm
Entry charge.

For a real history lesson, visit what lies below the city. Among the attractions are the tufa quarries that supplied the stone to build aqueducts and catacombs, and were later used as air-raid shelters and secret storehouses. A 90-minute tour with the Associazione Napoli Sotterranea will have many such revelations in store.

❺ Pizzeria 'The Three Tables'★★
Via Tribunali, 35
Cl. Sun.

This is a good place to have a meal. Though the restaurant is tiny, the owner Esterina is delightfully grumpy and the pizza crust is as soft and golden as can be. If you only want a snack, try the courgette flower fritters (*fiorilli*) that are sold at Di Matteo (no. 94) when in season. If you're not counting calories, try the delicious

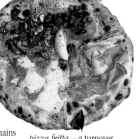

pizza fritta – a turnover made from pizza pastry, with ricotta cheese filling, fried in oil.

❻ Church of Santa Maria delle Anime del Purgatorio★★★
Via Tribunali, 35
Mon.-Sat. 11.30am-12.30pm.
Entry free.

At the entrance to the church there are three small columns, each surmounted by a bronze skull – hence the local name 'church of the skulls' – where carnations are laid every day. It was built in the 17th century, and its

❼ THE *VEILED CHRIST*★★★
Capella Sansevero
Via F. de Sanctis, 19
☎ 081 551 84 70
Every day 10am-5pm,
Tue. and Sun. 10am-1pm
Entry charge.

The statue of the veiled Christ is a remarkable masterpiece by the Neapolitan sculptor Sammartino, who used his technical prowess to give the marble the semblance of being covered by a veil, at once hiding and revealing the body of the inanimate Christ.

macabre distinguishing features are explained by the presence of an underground cemetery and ossuary. Here, well-preserved skulls stare out at you from alcoves – a reminder of the popular cult of the souls of Purgatory, a cult the Christian church stopped recognising in 1968.

Spaccanapoli, an open-air museum

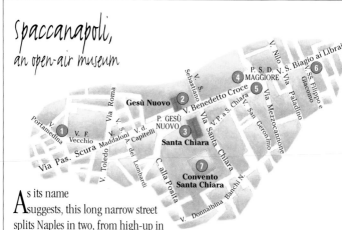

A s its name suggests, this long narrow street splits Naples in two, from high-up in the San Martino district down to the central station. Because of the number of churches and palaces along it, it has been likened to an 'open-air museum'. It's also one of the liveliest parts of the city, with many shops, craft workshops, buzzing university faculties and inviting café terraces.

❶ Montesanto market★★
Piazza and Via Pignasecca
Mon.-Sat. 9am-1.30pm.

The small Pignasecca market (very busy in the mornings) is a reminder that Spaccanapoli is a working class district where people continue to live. Amid the colourful stalls and smells of the sea, you may be lucky enough to hear the beautiful tenor voice of one of Naples' biggest fish vendors break into song.

❷ The Baroque Church of the Gesù Nuovo★★
Piazza del Gesù Nuovo
☎ 081 551 86 13
Every day 6.15am-12.45pm, 4.15-7.30pm
Entry free.

This Renaissance palace of the Sansevero princes was bought by the Jesuits in 1548, when it became the Church of Gesù Nuovo. It retains the original diamond-point embossed façade, and its colourful

marble interior will delight lovers of the Baroque. The thanksgiving chapel is a must.

❸ The Gothic Church of Santa Chiara★★★
Via Bendetto Croce
☎ 081 552 62 09
Every day 7am-12.30pm, 4-7pm. Entry free.

This church, with its pure Gothic lines, is in clear contrast to the Gesù Nuovo. It was rediscovered after the restoration work following the fire of 1943. The interior is spartan – as is typical of the Franciscan order, though the elegant tombs of Robert and Charles of Anjou and Marie de Valois by Da Camaiano serve as a reminder of the church's past royal connections. Fragments of frescoes by Giotto can be seen in the choir

of the Convento Santa Chiara. Some Neapolitans consider it *the* place to get married.

❹ Piazza San Domenico Maggiore★

This piazza was originally laid out during the Renaissance by the city's Aragonese rulers, and the aristocratic palaces around it were built later, in the 17th century. The monumental spire (*guglia*), erected at the end of the plague epidemic of 1656, is now a meeting place for students, singers, street performers and *bancarelle* (stalls). Access to the church of San Domenico Maggiore is gained via the monumental stairway leading into the apse. It's worth having a quick look inside just to see Caravaggio's *The Flagellation of Christ*.

❺ Patisserie Scaturchio★★

Piazza San Domenico Maggiore, 19
☎ 081 551 69 44
Every day exc. Tue.
7.20am-8.40pm.

Scaturchio has been a household name since the 19th century. Whether or not you're on a diet, try a *ministeriale* (mini or normal size) – a delicious medallion of delicate chocolate, with a cream and liqueur filling made from a secret recipe. Or if you prefer a quick coffee, try Bar Nilo, on Piazzetta Nilo. As you sip their excellent coffee, admire the statue of the God Nile, also known as the 'Body of Naples' as he symbolises the city.

❻ Jewellery and religious trinkets in San Biagio★

Via S. Biagio dei Llibrai, 81
☎ 081 20 30 67
Mon.-Sat.
10am-2pm,
4-8pm.

❼ An oasis of green★★★

Via S. Chiara, 49/C
☎ 081 552 62 80
Mon.-Sat. 8.30am-12.30pm, 3.30-6.30pm,
Sun. 9.30am-1pm.
Donation welcome.

Right in the heart of the busy city is the Convento Santa Chiara, its cloister nestling between large dormitory buildings. It's an oasis of peace, justifiably renowned for its garden and exquisite majolica tiling – all Mediterranean blues, yellows and greens. There's a wisteria-covered pergola under which to compose your thoughts with only the birds for company. Access is permitted on payment of a small donation.

Most jewellers and shops selling religious trinkets are located in the San Biagio area of Naples. Alongside the specialist workshops that make religious statues, you'll also come across a vast array of colourful kitsch versions of chalices, figurines and Madonnas. Perhaps your last port of call should be Luigi Grassi's famous Ospedale delle Bambole ('Dolls' Hospital'), where he restores old dolls, puppets and figurines with the greatest of skill.

The Spanish Quarter and Pizzofalcone

This is a little-known, much-talked-about part of Naples that combines a bad reputation with undeniable charm. From dawn onwards it's a hive of activity – full of voices and colours – with sudden surprising effects of sunlight on its piazzas and *vicoli*. A map shows the layout of the streets to be a series of small grids, yet the area has the feel of a labyrinth, with the darkest *bassi* and sunniest terraces. It starts in Via Roma and ends towards the hills of Sant'Elmo. Yet for all its industry, it has its quiet parts too.

❶ Spanish Quarter

This particular area was laid out in the middle of the 16th

century as part of a plan by the viceroy Don Pedro of Toledo to extend the city. At the same time as Via Toledo was extended, blocks of new housing were built for the troops in the west. These followed a rectangular layout that backed onto the hillside towards San Martino, and many of the streets end in a flight of stone stairs. Many of the bassi now reach onto the street because of illegal extensions. Other illegal constructions have meant that the same streets are taller than originally intended, and all the darker for it.

❷ A stroll★★★

To fully appreciate the life of this area just follow the slope of the streets, from the start of the Pedamantina steps in Montesanto down to the area around the Chiaia bridge, where a more aristocratic part of Naples begins. You'll stroll under balconies and past the workshops and small businesses that line the streets. You'll also come

across churches and the house where the poet Leopardi lived (Via Nuova S. Maria Ognibene, 52). A word of warning, though – be careful not to take any valuables with you on your walk.

❸ Palazzo Serra di Cassano★★★
Via Monte di Dio, 14-15
☎ 081 764 26 52
Mon.-Fri. 7.30am-7.30pm,
Sat. 7.30am-noon.

This palace's monumental stairway has all the hallmarks of the genius of Ferdinando Sanfelice and his baroque taste for dramatic, purely decorative features. The twin marble flights of stairs with trompe-l'oeil banisters lead up to the *piano nobile* (upper floor), which now houses the highly-respected Istituto per Gli Studi Filosofici.

❹ Pizzofalcone★★

It was on this rock in the shape of a falcon's (*falcone*) head, that Greek settlers founded Parthenope in the 7th century BC. It was reputedly named after the mermaid who allowed herself to die on the same shore. The settlement was renamed Paleapolis ('Old City') 200 years later, and forsaken until the 16th century, when it became a residential area for the Neapolitan aristocracy. Traces of Roman remains are still to be seen on the hillside. Be sure to enjoy the viewpoint at the end of Via Egiziaca.

❺ Via Toledo★

From the 17th century onwards, this main street was a favoured address for European aristocrats and bankers. The buildings continue to testify to this illustrious past: Palazzo Maddaloni (Via Maddaloni, 46), by Fanzago, is a very fine example of Baroque civic architecture, while Palazzo Doria D'Angri (Piazza VII Settembre) and Palazzo Berio (no.256) were built a century later by Vanvitelli. Nowadays Via Toledo still has numerous

banks, and perhaps most interesting is the interior of the Banca commerciale d'Italia.

❼ Church of Sant' Anna dei Lombardi★★
Piazza Monteoliveto 3
Tue.-Thu., Sat. 8.30am-12.30pm.

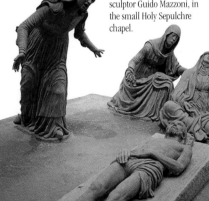

❻ Pintauro★
Via Toledo, 275.

At mere mention of Pintauro, most Neapolitan taste-buds will start to water – Pintauro is the undisputed king of the *sfogliatella* (see p. 22). On these ancient premises you'll always find, just out of the oven, warm *sfogliatelle*, either plain *frolla* or *riccia*, shaped like a seashell. Both are delicious.

Work on this church first started in 1411, and it was here that the Aragon rulers came to pray. The many chapels (Tolosa, Terranova and Piccolomini) were decorated by the greatest Italian artists of the day, and contain a wealth of treasure. Of particular note are the frescoes by Vasari (in the Sagrestia Vecchia), the *Annunciation* by Da Maiano (in the Cappella Curiale) and the *Lamentation over the Dead Christ*, a set of life-size terracotta statues by the sculptor Guido Mazzoni, in the small Holy Sepulchre chapel.

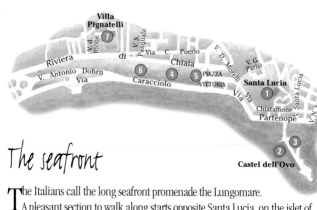

Villa
Pignatelli
7

V. d. Rione · V. S. Pasquale · C. Poerio · V. D. Morelli · V. G. Parisi

Riviera · di · Chiaia

V. Antonio Dohrn · Via · **6** · Via · **4** · **5** · PIAZZA VITTORIA

Caracciolo · Santa Lucia · **1**

Via Santa Lucia · V. N. Sauro

Chiatamone
Partenope

2
3

Castel dell'Ovo

The seafront

The Italians call the long seafront promenade the Lungomare.
A pleasant section to walk along starts opposite Santa Lucia, on the islet of Megaris (whose tip divides the Bay of Naples) and ends at the Villa Communale park. In between, you follow the curve of Via Caracciolo, which offers a wonderful view of the Bay. It's a section of Naples that changes distinctly, not only according to the season but also according to the time of the day.

❶ Santa Lucia★★

Until the 16th century, Santa Lucia was the name of a beach and small fishing village. Then, in 1599, the viceroy Enriquez de Guzman, the Count of Olivares, ordered the construction of a main road, as part of a plan to transform the area and extend the city to the west. It was only fully completed in the 20th century, when tower blocks were put up between the sea and the coast road. Santa Lucia is now one of Naples' best-known streets and the location of most of the luxury hotels, including the famous Vesuvio.

❷ Castel dell'Ovo★★★
Open for cultural events.

The city's oldest castle, the so-called 'Castle of the Egg', stands on the islet of Megaris. According to medieval legend, the castle had links with the poet Virgil, and one of his lucky charms lies hidden in the castle foundations. The charm is said to be an egg kept in a bottle, itself protected by a small metal cage. For as long as the egg remains intact, Naples need fear neither destruction nor invasion. The castle terrace offers a breathtaking view of the city, sea and Bay.

❸ The *Tabaccaio* in the Borgo Marinaro★★★
☎ 081 764 63 52

Open lunchtime and evening, Closed Thu.

At the foot of the castle is the Borgo Marinaro, which was once a fishing village and is now a marina. Despite all the restaurant terraces, it's easy to spot the modest sign of the Tabaccaio. It's called *tabaccaio* because it's not only a restaurant but also a tobacconist's. It's a good place to come and try Rosario's *spaghetti alla Conte*, made with shrimps and Mediterranean prawns (L12,000), right in the marina looking onto the luxury hotels.

❹ Villa Comunale★★

The Villa Comunale is one of the city's few parks. Lodged between the Via Caracciolo to the south and the Riviera di Chiaia to the north, it's an area with trees and the occasional statue, where parents often come with their children and there's space enough to kick a football around. It was Ferdinand IV who first conceived the idea of making it into a public park, and he entrusted the work to the architect Vanvitelli and landscape gardener Abbate. The entire expanse of the park is a reclaimed area that was once swampy woodland.

❺ H. Production★★
Piazza Vittoria
Open all year, weather permitting.

H. Production rents out unusual quadricycles (seating up to six), and has its 'headquarters' at the main entrance to Villa Comunale, in Piazza Vittoria. The cycles are an excellent way of seeing the 18th and 19th-century statues and elegant Art Nouveau bandstand that decorate the park at your leisure. Half an hour costs around L7,000.

❻ Stazione Zoologica A. Dohrn and aquarium★★★
Villa Comunale
Tue.-Sat. 9am-5pm, Sun. and holidays 9am-2pm.
Entry charge.

Both the marine biology research institute and aquarium are housed in an unrenovated 19th-century building. In other respects too, Naples' tiny aquarium – the oldest in Europe – must seem a poor cousin to its European and American counterparts. It has 25 tanks, containing specimens of the flora and fauna of the Bay of Naples in their natural environment, i.e. about 200 different species.

❼ PIGNATELLI VILLA AND MUSEUM★
Riviera di Chiaia, 200
Tue.-Sat. 9am-2pm, Sun. 9am-1pm.
Entry charge.

It's hard to miss the imposing neo-Doric colonnade forming part of the façade of the Diego Aragona Pignatelli Cortes museum. The villa-museum was designed along the lines of an old Pompeiian town house and is set in a beautiful English-style garden, with several picturesque outbuildings – a neo-Gothic tower, a Swiss chalet and a greenhouse, one of which houses the Carriage Museum. The villa is often used for temporary exhibitions, concerts and other cultural events.

The heart of the old capital

This area was once the heart of the Kingdom of Naples and the Two Sicilies.

The most important buildings of the then-capital — castles, theatres, palaces and lavish private residences — were all concentrated around Piazza Plebiscito and Piazza Municipio, in what is today a small area open to the sea..

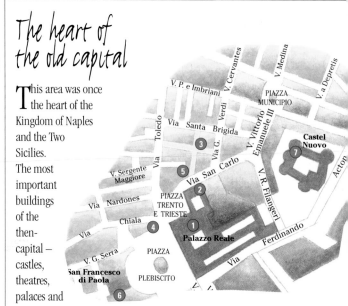

❶ Palazzo Reale★★★

Piazza Plebiscito
☎ 081 580 81 11
Open every day 9.30am-10pm (until 8pm Sun. and hols.)
Entry charge.

The palace, originally intended for a visit by King Ferdinand III of Spain, was started in 1600 but only completed three centuries later. Statues of the eight kings of Naples are set into

recesses along the façade, and give the curious impression of standing guard. Inside the palace is a labyrinth of stairways, private rooms, corridors, gardens, terraces and inner courtyards. If, after this mini-marathon, you're in need of sustenance, try Aldo Bruno, whose cafetaria is in the grounds of the palace and offers excellent value for money (L15,000-20,000).

❷ Teatro San Carlo★★★

Via San Carlo, 93/f
☎ 081 797 21 11/081 714 57 37 (guided tours).

The Teatro San Carlo, built in 1737 in honour of Charles III, soon established

itself as one of the world's leading opera houses. Bellini's *La Sonnambula* premiered here. It's certainly worth coming if you have the opportunity, and ballet, opera or concert tickets are often available even on the day of the performance. Tickets usually cost L60,000-160,000. The theatre is also open to visitors during the day, though visiting hours often vary, so phone first.

❸ Galleria Umberto★

Entrances in Via Roma and Via Verdi.

This glass-roofed arcade was built in 1890 to meet two needs: to regenerate the Santa Brigida area (after the 1884 cholera

epidemic) and to provide the city with an emblem of modern industrial civilisation. The four wings of the gallery are laid out in the direction of the compass points and meet in a central glass cupola (57m/187ft). This impressive iron-and-glass structure lets in plenty of light. Inside are shops and cafés. By contrast with neighbouring streets, the peace and tranquillity here seem almost provincial.

4 Café Gambrinus★★
Piazza Trieste e Trento, 38
☎ 081 41 75 82.

The Gambrinus, with its Art Nouveau decor, is the most famous café in Naples. Along with the Florian in Venice and the Greco in Rome, it belongs to the Italian café association. Over the years, it has had numerous famous clients (among them Verdi and the writer Gabriele D'Annunzio), and is now also a patisserie/ice-cream

parlour/tea-room. It's an ideal place to come for a coffee or aperitif. The Gambrinus is, of course, packed with tourists in summer, though it's popular with Neapolitans too.

5 Shoe-shiners★★★
Galleria Umberto
Mon.-Sat. 8.30am-2.30pm.

Opposite the celebrated San Carlo theatre is a locally-famous (and unique) *lustrascarpe* (shoe-shine) business. Antonio and Gennaro, 73 and 70 respectively, are the last in the line of a slowly-dying but proud tradition. Don't worry if you feel embarrassed about someone else cleaning your shoes – both Antonio and Gennaro will tell you it's a job like any other. A shoe-shine costs L5,000-10,000, depending on the kind of shoe.

6 Church of San Francesco di Paola★
Every day
8am-noon, 3-6pm.

Piazza Plebiscito, alongside the Palazzo Reale, has long been the site of military parades, public festivities and concerts, as well as a place for walks. The Church of

San Francesco di Paola in the centre of the piazza, 34m/112ft wide and rising 53m/174ft from a circular base, is reminiscent in both form and size of the Pantheon in Rome – and is flanked by a colonnade.

7 CASTEL NUOVO★
Piazza Municipio
☎ 081 795 20 03
Mon.-Sat. 9am-7pm.
Entry charge.

Castel Nuovo, also known as the Maschio Angioino, is the fortress whose severe bulk and five imposing towers dwarf Piazza Municipio. The ornate triumphal arch adorning the entrance commemorates the victory of the armies of Alphonse V of Spain over the Angevins. A flower market is held every morning in the castle moat. (see p.112).

Vomero

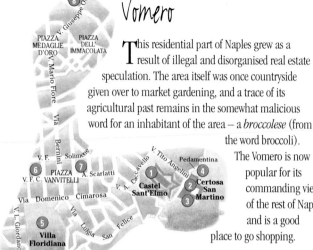

PIAZZA MEDAGLIE D'ORO
PIAZZA DELL' IMMACOLATA
V. Mario Fiore
V. Giuseppe Orsi **8**

V. F. Solimene
Bernini
V. F. C. VANVITELLI **6**
PIAZZA VANVITELLI
A. Scarlatti **7**
Via Domenico Cimarosa
V. A. Caccavello
V. Tito Angelini
Pedamentina
1 Castel Sant'Elmo
4 Certosa San Martino **2** **3**
V. L. Giordano
Via Luigia
San Felice
5 Villa Floridiana

This residential part of Naples grew as a result of illegal and disorganised real estate speculation. The area itself was once countryside given over to market gardening, and a trace of its agricultural past remains in the somewhat malicious word for an inhabitant of the area – a *broccolese* (from the word broccoli).

The Vomero is now popular for its commanding views of the rest of Naples, and is a good place to go shopping.

❶ Castel Sant'Elmo★★

Largo S. Martino
☎ **081 578 40 30**
Tue.-Sun. 9am-2pm.
Entry charge.

This castle was started in the 14th century by the Angevin rulers, but only took on its present-day star shape two centuries later. Because of its strategic position, the Viceroy of Toledo made the castle the centre of the city's defence system. Though used for a long time as a prison, it's nowadays a more welcoming place and offers a superb panoramic view of the Bay.

❷ Certosa San Martino★★★

Largo S. Martino
☎ **081 578 17 69**
Tue.-Sun. 9am-2pm.
Entry charge.

MVSEO NAZIONALE DI S MARTINO

This charterhouse has been a museum since the unification of Italy in 1860. Though first built in the 14th century, the building itself is now a fine example of the Neapolitan Baroque. The interior was decorated by well-known artists – make sure you see the works of Vaccaro and Ribera in the church. The cloister and step terraces are the perfect place for a pause.

❸ The Neapolitan crib scenes★★★

Same opening times as the Certosa San Martino.

The section containing Neapolitan art is housed in what were once the convent kitchens. The play of light changes dramatically throughout the day, recreating the passage of day into night. The central piece of the collection is a large-scale 18th-century crib that belonged to the collector and playwright Cucciniello. Another notable figurine is the *Blind Beggar* by Sammartino, the artist who sculpted the *Veiled Christ* (see p.39).

❹ The Pedamentina★★★

The *pedementina* is a series of 414 steps leading down from the esplanade in front of

the castle into the heart of Naples. Each successive bend in the path throws up new insights into the city – some as innocently intimate as a cat lazing in the sunshine or a forgotten building – and its bucolic atmosphere seems far removed from the frenzy of Naples.

5 Villa Floridiana★

Via D. Cimarosa, 77
☎ 081 578 84 18
(museum)
Villa 9am-one hour
before sunset,
museum Tue.-Sun.
9am-1pm.
Entry charge
for museum.

The Villa Floridiana was bought by the Bourbon King Ferdinand I for his second wife, and redesigned in the neo-Classical style in the mid-19th century. Set in the villa's grounds – a delightful succession of pines, cypresses, ilexes and attractive gazebos – is the Duca di Martina museum, which houses one of the finest

collections of Italian decorative arts, especially pottery and ceramics.

6 Via Scarlatti★

This pedestrian street is ideal for shopping. Lined with plane trees, it's an almost uninterrupted row of temptations, especially clothes. You'll also find department stores and the Scarlatti and Vanvitelli shopping arcades. The intersection with Via Luca Giordano is a popular meeting-place for young Neapolitans.

7 Glacier Soave★★

Via Scarlatti, 130
☎ 081 556 74 11
Mon.-Sat.
8am-1.30pm, 4.30-7pm.

Take a break from shopping and stop in at Soave for a cornetto . They have all flavours, from traditional to seasonal (such as chestnut in winter or fruits of the forest in summer). Cornettos cost L2,000-3,500. The chocolate-rimmed sort is excellent.

8 LELLO ESPOSITO'S WORKSHOP★★

Salita Arenella, 56
☎ 081 578 64 50.

This is where the masked character Pulcinella can be found in multiple guises (in terracotta or bronze). The creations are the work of Lello Esposito, an artist and craftsman who stopped mass-producing works to concentrate on almost life-size sculptures, and whose work has been exhibited in the Pompidou Centre in Paris. It's best to telephone first to make sure the workshop is open, as Signor Esposito comes and goes as he pleases. Prices start from L30,000. Note, too, that the workshop is expected to move to Piazza S. Domenico Maggiore in the near future. .

The Sanità district

Since ancient times, the area north of the old city walls has been used as a burial ground and a place to worship the dead. Though nowadays a seemingly normal working-class area full of bustle, it's one of the most mysterious parts of Naples, and a must if you like intriguing places.

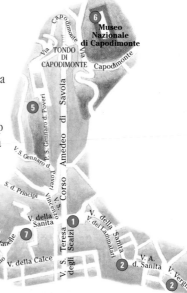

❶ Via Sanità★

Via Sanità is in the heart of this enclosed area. From the Sanità bridge crossing Via Sanità you can see how the area lies at the foot of the higher and more salubrious Capodimonte district. Along the street are aristocratic façades and churches, squeezed between

modest-looking buildings housing small businesses and shops, including the famous *taralli* sellers.

❷ Palazzo San Felice★★★
Via Sanità, 2/6
Open holidays only
9am-6pm. Entry free.

Ferdinando Sanfelice built the imposing and original Palazzo San Felice for his family in

1728. Built in the Baroque style, it includes a 'hawk-wing' staircase (so named because of its form), the style of which was copied a decade later in the nearby Palazzo dello Spagnolo (Via Vergini, 19). It's worth going inside to find out more about the palace's unusual layout, and to visit the garden at the rear.

❸ La Cantina del Gallo★
Via Telesino
Closed Sun.

The man behind this very popular

restaurant is Mario. His speciality is *saltimbocca* (literally 'jump in your mouths'), small turnovers made with pizza pastry and peppers, aubergines, *friarelli* sausages or *ricotta* cheese. Mario may also bring you *gnochetti* or marinated anchovies to complete your meal. While you're waiting, ask to see the car park which has been carved out of the volcanic cliffside. Expect to pay L20,000-25,000 for a meal.

❹ Fontanelle Cemetery★★★
Via Fontanelle, 77
Temporarily closed for restoration.

This cemetery has its own unique atmosphere, as befits a meeting-place between the worlds of the living and the dead. Here you'll see thousands of skulls and other bones belonging to unknown dead that are now tended by their 'adopted families'. This is done in return for protection and the answering of prayers.

❺ San Gennaro catacombs★★
Via Capodimonte,13
☎ 081 741 10 71
Guided tours every day at 9.30am, 10.15am, 11am and 11.45am. Entry charge.

The catacombs date from the 3rd century, and it was here that the mortal remains of the martyred bishop of Naples, San Gennaro, were placed in the 5th century, until their later removal to the Duomo. The catacombs comprise large rooms over two levels, with paintings and mosaics on the walls, and are among the most important early Christian burial sites. The fresco of San Gennaro is probably the city's oldest image of its patron saint.

❻ Museo Nazionale di Capodimonte★★
Via Miano, 2
☎ 081 744 13 07
Tue.-Sat. 10am-10pm, Sun. 10am-8pm.

Set amid greenery, this art gallery is housed in the royal palace built by the Bourbon King Charles III when Naples became the capital of the Kingdom of the Two Sicilies.

The large Farnese collection was brought here and added to, and the museum holds an exceptional anthology of Italian painting (including Caravaggio, Correggio and Lotto) and Flemish painting (Pieter Brueghel). The Portrait of *Antea* by Parmigianino is very fine. Have a look, too, at Queen Maria Amalia's unusual porcelain parlour, and the collection of modern art.

❼ LOCAL HEROES★

The walls of Via Sanità are covered with vivid posters of international stars and the best-known Neapolitan singers (complete with fixed grins and blow-dried hair). There's a mural of Maradona, who for Neapolitans has never fallen from the rank of living god, alongside no. 87. An equally popular figure is the famous comic actor Totò. He was born in the area, and his house is now a mini-museum. He's said to have slipped out at night to push money under the doors of the neighbourhood's poorest families.

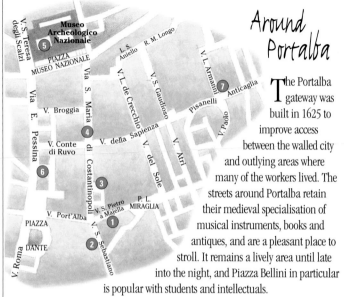

Around Portalba

The Portalba gateway was built in 1625 to improve access between the walled city and outlying areas where many of the workers lived. The streets around Portalba retain their medieval specialisation of musical instruments, books and antiques, and are a pleasant place to stroll. It remains a lively area until late into the night, and Piazza Bellini in particular is popular with students and intellectuals.

❶ Colonnese bookshop★★

Via S. Pietro a Maiella, 32-33
☎ **081 45 98 58**
Mon.-Fri. 9am-1pm, 4-7.30pm, Sat. 9am-1.30pm.

There are many new and secondhand bookshops in the Via Portalba, between Piazza Dante and Piazza Bellini. A little further down in the Via San Pietro a Maiella is the Colonnese bookshop. It differs from

most bookshops in that Gaetano and Maria not only publish interesting works, they also hold exhibitions and talks. The Colonnese is a hushed place, also selling many postcards, illustrations and other intriguing items – always in good condition.

❷ Via San Sebastiano★★

This street close to the famous San Pietro a Maiella Conservatoire is a favourite with musicians. The shops here sell specialised books, rare musical scores and musical bibliographies, as well as musical instruments. If you're in the area, drop into the conservatoire to admire its very attractive courtyard (Via S. Pietro a Maiella, 4, entry free).

❸ Piazza Bellini★★★

Piazza Bellini is on the edge of the original town, and remains of a 4th-century BC perimeter wall can still be seen. Since its recent renovation and new status as a pedestrian area, the piazza has become a popular spot. People often arrange to meet at the foot of the statue of Vincenzo Bellini. Whether it's to have a drink or snack, or to chat under the wisteria, there's a café for everyone – bookshop café,

Internet café or Arabian café. To get a table in summer, it's best to arrive before 11pm.

❹ Via Costantinopoli★★

Walking from Piazza Bellini to the National Archaeology Museum, takes you past the antique shops in Via Santa Maria di Constantinopoli. Each has its own speciality, i.e. sculpture, prints, furniture, porcelains or bronzes. L'Antiquario, at no. 34, is the oldest shop in the street, and offers the widest selection to choose from. Every second Sunday in the month, traders display their wares on the street.

It's as well not to expect a bargain – Italians are fiercely possessive of their heritage and know its true value.

❺ Museo Archeologico Nazionale★★★

Piazza Museo, 35
☎ 081 44 01 66
Every day exc. Tue.
10am-10pm.
Entry charge.

This specialist museum has one of the largest collections of Greek and Roman artefacts in the world. A clear insight into daily life in Pompeii and Herculaneum can be gained through the collections of delicately-crafted jewellery, vases, cameos and glasswork. There are also excellently-preserved mosaics. Overall, the museum traces the development of Mediterranean civilisation from the Etruscan era through to Roman times. It's a must, even if you're not mad on old stones.

❼ Via Anticaglia★★

This is another *decumanus* (a Roman east-west road), though nowadays it's neither as straight nor as busy as the other two. It owes its charm to the arches that cross it. In Greek and Roman times, these allowed access from the baths to the theatre. From this street, you can reach the Pharmacy of the Incurables, in the hospital of the same name (Ospedale degli Incurabili). The pharmacy is only open in May. It contains fine walnut furnishings, and 400 or so

❻ Adela Impronta★

Via C. Doria, 8
☎ 081 544 97 53
Mon.-Fri.
10am-1.30pm, 4.30-8pm,
Sat. 10am-1.30pm.

Adela, the owner, produces all types, sizes and colours of candles – decorative, scented, designed to remove cigarette smoke, esoteric and even votive. Adela's son, Luigi, can also make up candles according to your specifications. If you're superstitious, you may find it useful to know the shop also sells a range of talismens, magic charms, and books on how to ward off the evil eye. Traditional candles sell for L5,000-30,000, whereas decorative candles can cost as much as L400,000.

medicinal jars, each decorated with different scenes and motifs, so that illiterate assistants could tell the contents.

From Mergellina to Posillipo

Without doubt one of the most attractive places in Naples is the Posillipo hill, with the small port of Mergellina nestling at its foot. The best way to visit the area is to take the 140 bus in Mergellina and alight at the end of the route in Capo Posillipo. You can then walk back down the hill, admiring the view at your leisure.

❶ *Taralli caldi*★

The Neapolitan speciality *taralli caldi* are small ring-shaped biscuits made from flour, water, pork fat, almonds and pepper. These salty and spicy biscuits go well with a glass of beer and make an ideal snack as you walk along the seafront. They're sold in Via Carracciolo, Via Mergellina and the port area, usually from stalls that sell them warm (a small bag costs L500).

❷ Mergellina 'chalets'★

The Mergellina 'chalets' are in fact not chalets but small kiosks selling ice cream, located opposite the *taralli caldi* stalls.

It's customary to stop here on a Sunday afternoon walk to have one of the delicious homemade ice-creams, *frullatti* (milkshakes) made from exotic fruits (L7,000) or fruit salads. Chalet Ciro in Mergellina is one of the best-known of these popular establishments.

❸ Bagno Elena★
Via Posillipo, 14
☎ 081 575 50 58.

The easiest way to have a swim in Naples is probably to come here. Inside a small bay at the entrance to the Via Posillipo, Bagno Elena provides everything you need to while away the time

pleasantly. The setting is beautiful, with Vesuvius on one side, Palazzo Donn'Anna on the other, and the island of Capri opposite. Admission costs L9,000, and you have the choice of a parasol (L5,000), beachbed (L7,000) or deckchair (L5,000). Arrive before 9am if you want to be sure of avoiding the crowds and finding a good spot in summer.

❹ Palazzo Donn'Anna★★
Via Posillipo.

The Palazzo Donn'Anna, which owes its name to Donn'Anna Carafa di

Stigliano, stands right at the water's edge. Work on it started in 1637, following Donn'Anna's marriage, but was never completed. Since then, the palace has been abandoned, ransacked and redesigned, yet its tall open windows continue to give it the look of a haunted building. Having also given rise to many local legends, and no doubt silently witnessed forbidden love affairs and horrible deaths, it's become one of the city's landmarks.

❺ Piazza San Luigi and Bilancione★
☎ 081 769 19 23
Every day except Wed.
7am–midnight.

Piazza San Luigi is a vast open space in the shape of an amphitheatre, and a popular spot with Posillipo's night owls. Very near here, the Bilancione ice-cream

parlour, run by two brothers of the same name who've been making ice-cream for 20 years, offers a bewildering choice of 50 different flavours. The most famous of these is hazelnut. With your ice-cream in your hand, all you need to do is cross the road and go and sit on one of the public benches to savour both the ice-cream and the setting.

❻ Marechiaro★★★
Ask the bus driver to drop you at the start of the road that leads down to Marechiaro (which means, approximately, 'where the sea is calm'). This charming spot is famous locally for the story of a young Neapolitan girl, Carolina, who used to lean out of her window to

hear her sweetheart serenading her down below.

Since then, the tale has been immortalised in the now-classic Neapolitan song, *Marechiaro*.

❼ Views of the Bay of Naples★★★
The whole of Via Posillipo offers splendid views of the Bay of Naples as far as Capo Posillipo. From Piazza Salvatore di Giacomo, follow the sinuous Via Ferdinando Russo, lined with sumptuous villas, down to the sea. Neapolitans call this spot Giuseppone a Mare, the name of a local restaurant. Perched there on the rocks, you'll see it's a charming place to relax.

❽ THE PARCO VIRGILIANO, OR PARCO DELLA RIMEMBRANZA★★★
Though everyone will tell you the park is closed to the public, it's nevertheless possible to squeeze through gaps in the railings. If you're prepared to go through with this minor breach of the law, you'll have a unique 180° view of the Bay of Naples and Bay of Pozzuoli, with the islands of Procida, Ischia and Capri in the distance.

Pompeii and Herculaneum

On 24 August AD 79 the eruption of Vesuvius destroyed both Pompeii and the nearby town of Herculaneum. Pompeii was buried under a thick layer of ash and cinders, and Herculaneum was submerged under flows of molten lava and mud – which explains why Herculaneum was found better preserved than Pompeii when the two sites were rediscovered in the 18th century and archeological work began.

POMPEII

❶ Forum★★
The site of Pompeii is open every day, 9am-one hour before sunset.
Entry charge.

The forum is a rectangular public space, measuring 38m/125ft by 142m/465ft enclosed on three sides by a portico. As this was once the centre of all political, religious, economic and legal life, it's also where most of Pompeii's important buildings are to be found, including the Temples of Apollo and Jupiter, the *macellum* (a large covered market), where

meat, fish, fresh vegetables and basil were sold, and, perhaps most important of all, the courthouse.

❷ Daily life

To have a better idea of daily life in Pompeii, visit the **Stabian Baths★★★**, which are probably the oldest public baths in the city. There was a section for men and another for women, each with its own changing rooms and series of rooms with cold, tepid and hot-water baths.
The House of Vettii★★, once owned by rich

merchants, is also worth a look, as it still has exceptionally well-preserved frescoes, including the one on the wall in the hallway depicting Priapus weighing his enormous phallus.

❸ The brothel★★★
The best-preserved example of a Pompeian brothel is to be found behind the public baths. In its day, it contained 10 rooms, five of which were on the first floor reached by a small stairway. Each small room had a bed and stone bolster and a wooden door.

The walls were decorated with unashamedly erotic scenes, no doubt depicting the services offered by the prostitutes and servants.

❹ The Amphitheatre★★★

The amphitheatre, located in the easternmost section of the city, was built in 80 BC, and is today considered

to be one of the oldest of its kind in the world. It was built in stages, with terraces progressively supported by ground taken from the arena, which explains why the latter is below the level of the city square and has no underground passages.

❺ Via dei Sepolcri and Villa dei Misteri★★★

The best example of a necropolis in Pompeii is Via dei Sepolcri ('street of the tombs'), a street lined on either side by funerary monuments, that leads up to the Villa dei Misteri outside the city walls. The Villa dei Misteri ('Villa of the Mysteries') was once an aristocratic villa, and owes its renown to its frescoes. This set of 29 life-sized figures depicts a young bride's initiation into the mysteries

❻ A shortcut from old to new Pompeii★

Once you reach the site of the amphitheatre in old Pompeii, you can leave the historic city through the Piazza Anfiteatro and Via Roma and enter modern Pompeii. Here, on the square in front of the cathedral, you'll find ice-cream parlours and bars. If you arrived by train from Naples, there's a station on the Circumvesuviana line (see p. 33) close by.

of Dionysus, the god of vine, wine and ecstasy.

HERCULANEUM

❼ The Trellis House (Graticcio)★★★

The name comes from the wooden structures that form the skeleton of the walls. The building is a well-preserved example of humble living accommodation, and contains two separate

apartments. Some of the rooms were probably rented. It's the only example of inexpensive architecture that remains.

❽ The House with the Mosaic Atrium★★

The name comes from the black and white chessboard pattern of the mosaic in the atrium. The uneven surface of the ground was caused by the weight of the lava flows. The house once had a fine view of the sea. From the terrace, the wall of lava that now obstructs the view begins to give an idea of the height of the lava flows (up to 25m/80ft).

❾ The Resina market★★

If you're looking for leather clothes, then you might find what you want at the flea market in Resina, the modern-day Herculaneum. The shirt and jacket section is usually the most rewarding. Otherwise, you'll have to rummage through mounds of different styles of clothes at different prices. It's also worth looking at the household linen, where there are often bargains to be had.

Salerno and Paestum

It's easy to form the wrong impression and feel a little disappointed when you first arrive in Salerno. Despite the beauty of the Lungomare Trieste, it appears to be just another modern town. But you'd be wrong – the origins of the town by the sea (*salum*) with the river Irno running through it can be traced back to the 7th century BC. It first rose to prominence under Norman rule after 1077 and remained important right up to the 13th century. At that time, its faculty of medicine was the oldest and most renowned in Europe.

❶ Medieval centre★★

Salerno's fortified medieval centre clings to the hillside, and is lorded over by the Arechi Castle. It still has its original walls and many convents. The centre is a delight to explore on foot – whether around the attractive Piazza Luciani with its *loggie* and colourful terraces, or through narrow winding streets, taking in the crafts on display in Via Portacatena and Via dei Mercanti. Continuing in this direction will lead you to the very pretty Baroque church and cathedral of San Giorgio.

❷ Duomo and Diocesan Museum★★★

Piazza Alfano 1er
Every day 9am-1pm, 4-7pm.

Despite subsequent restoration work that has given it a Baroque or neo-Classical exterior, the cathedral, which dates back to 1080, is one of the finest examples of the southern Italian Romanesque. The colonnaded entrance hall at the top of the staircase houses the superb 11th-

century Porta dei leoni (Lion Door), while Arab influence is evident in the Romanesque arcade and bell-tower (1137-1145). The lecterns flanking the central nave predate the 18th-century alterations, and are in fact 12th-century originals. Make sure you also visit the museum, as it holds one of the richest collections of 12th-century ivory panels.

❸ Paestum★
Site open every day 9am-one hour before sunset. Entry charge.

It's something of a miracle that the three temples in Paestum survived until their discovery in the 18th century without having become a source of building materials for later generations and civilisations. It was originally a Greek settlement called Poseidonia (7th century BC), but later took the Roman name Paestum (273 BC). In the course of its history, the town was gradually abandoned in favour of sites further up the hillside and away from the recurrent dangers of malaria. This explains why the buildings (such as the agora, amphitheatre and forum) are so well preserved, as they haven't had to make

way for later additions. On fine days, the golden tinge of the chalk in the stone of the temples lends the scene a certain mystery.

❹ Temple of Ceres★
The many votive offerings discovered nearby prove that this temple was in fact dedicated to Athena and not Ceres. The temple is the smallest of the three, and was built around 500 BC. It was built in the Doric style, though there are Ionian touches, such as the capitals of the façade.

❺ Temples of Hera and Neptune★★
The Temple of Hera, the basilica, is the oldest (530 BC) of the three. The ancient style of its capitals and the 'swelling' of the columns initially led archaeologists to believe the temple was a civic building. The 'Temple to Neptune' (in fact, this too was dedicated to the cult of Hera) complied with the standards of classical architecture. Its form and elegance recall the most beautiful Greek monuments of the Classical era, especially the Parthenon, though this was built at a later date.

❻ Tomb of the Diver★★
**Museo Nazionale
Every day 9am-6.30pm.**

The lid of the tomb shows a diver, whose leap symbolises the passage into the afterlife. The four remaining slabs depict a funeral banquet. Apart from the excellent detail (particularly on the lid), the discovery of the tomb in 1968 was all the more significant as it turned out to be a unique example of Greek funerary painting of the period (c. 480 BC). There are also ceramics found in Paestum.

❼ THE BEACHES OF CILENTO★★

The area around Agropoli and Paestum provides opportunities for diving and is particularly pleasant from spring onwards. In summer, both S. Maria di Castellabate and Agropoli, whose houses seem to grow directly out of the hillside, are popular summer resorts, not least for their long sandy beaches.

The Amalfi coast

Ravello **⑥** Minori Maiori
N163
②③④
Positano Amalfi
⑦
Conca dei Marini
⑤
G. d. Smeraldo
Praiano

Breathtaking views await you at almost every turn of the coast road from Amalfi to Positano – a cliff rising steeply out of the sea or a small village nestling against the rock, all amid lush Mediterranean vegetation. It's heavenly, though on Saturdays and Sundays when the traffic is heavy, another word springs to mind.

❶ Cruise in the Bay of Naples★★★
Port de Molo Beverello
☎ **081 552 07 63**
Departing 9am, returning 6.30pm. Booking essential.

The company Navigazione Libera del Golfo offers a number of routes. The Blue Route includes an excursion to Capri and a chance to swim in the Faraglioni (s ee p.64). Then the journey continues along the Amalfi coast, with a 2-hour stop in Amalfi,

after which the boat skirts the Sorrento coast before heading back to Naples. All in all, an interesting way to see the Bay (L36,000).

❷ Cathedral of Sant'Andrea★★
Piazza Duomo
Every day 9am-1pm, 3-8pm.

The cathedral, or Duomo, built in the 9th century, is dedicated to Sant'Andrea, patron saint of the town. It has undergone

successive alterations in the past, and the mosaics and interlaced arches of the façade recall Arab-Byzantine influences. Access to the 13th-century Paradise Cloister is through the cathedral. The

Ferry departure point for the Bay of Naples, the islands and the Amalfi coast in the heart of the city

cloister was a burial ground for the Neapolitan aristocracy, and was intended to open the gates of heaven to those who had just died.

❸ Il Limoncello d'Amalfi★

Via L. d'Amalfi, 3
☎ 089 87 16 39
Every day in summer 9am-11pm, Nov.-Mar. 9am-1pm, 4-8.30pm.

This shop provides a good example of all that can be done with lemons. Of

course, lemons here are most famously used to produce *limoncello*, a lemon liqueur (L18,000 for 75cl), but you'll also find plenty of other ideas for lemon-based gifts – soaps, perfume, oil, candles, jams and much more.

❹ Carta d'Amalfi★★

When it was a maritime republic ranking alongside Venice or Palermo, Amalfi was renowned for its master

papermakers. The production methods haven't changed since the Middle Ages and remain the preserve of craftsmen. Authentic Amalfi paper bears the coat of arms of the ancient republic and a watermark – a nice change from postcards!

❺ Emerald Grotto★★★

One of the most surprising features of the coastline is to be found 4km/2½ miles from Amalfi, between Praiano and Conca dei Marini. The Emerald Grotto is in fact a large semi-underwater cave whose name and special colour derive from the effect of daylight filtering through an opening in the rock into the cave's enclosed pool of water. You can also witness the unusual spectacle of stalactites and stalagmites seemingly touching the surface of the water here.

❻ Ravello★★★

From Amalfi, a panoramic route winds its way steeply up to Ravello. This small village, off the beaten tourist track, was once part of the Duchy of Amalfi, and though not

❼ Positano★★★

With its many small houses closely dotted on the hillside down to the sea, Positano looks a little like one of the Neapolitan crib scenes. It was once a small fishing village, but today is world-famous as a seaside resort. Amid the gardens and hanging terraces are stairways and narrow alleys, all leading down to the beaches. If you go to Positano you'll see Positano fashions – baggy clothes with abstract designs and fluorescent colours and sandals – on sale everywhere.

easy to reach, it offers unparalleled views of the Amalfi coast. The terraced gardens of the Villa Rufolo and Villa Cimbrone, both of which are over 300m/980ft above sea level, are the best spots.

Sorrento

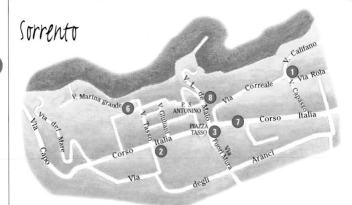

The town of Sorrento is one of the world's most famous resorts, and has also given its name to the coast. Its popularity dates back to ancient times, when the Romans were known to appreciate it for the mildness of its climate and the beauty of the setting. Nowadays, Sorrento also has much to offer in the way of local crafts and gastronomy.

❶ Correale di Terranova Museum★★★

Via Correale, 50
☎ **081 878 18 46**
Open every day exc. Tue. and holidays, 9am-2pm. Entry charge.

The museum is housed in an attractive 18th-century building and holds the collections of Alfredo and Pompeo Correale, the Counts of Terranova. The key exhibit is the Sorrento marquetry on display on the ground floor. After your visit, step into

the lovely garden planted with rare flowers and trees. A path lined with orange trees leads to the belvedere overlooking the Mediterranean and Sorrento coastline. To reach the museum from Piazza Tasso, follow Via Correale.

❷ Duomo★★

Via S. Maria della pietà, 44 /Corso Italia
☎ **081 878 12 44**
Every day 8am-noon, 3-10pm. Entry free.

This Romanesque cathedral dates back to the early 15th century, though the façade was completely remodelled in 1924. The interior houses paintings by the Neapolitan school (18th century) as well as the marble archbishop's throne (1573). Ancient Roman columns support the bell-tower, while the large multicoloured ceramic clock is the work of more recent local craftsmen.

❸ Bagni della Regina Giovanna★★★

From Piazza Tasso, a Sita bus service goes to Capo di Sorrento. From the small village of Capo, a shady narrow road leads steeply down to the coast. The Bagni della Regina Giovanna are situated at the end of the rocky promontory. The Bagni (Baths) are in fact a natural outdoor swimming pool in the form of a triangle. Steps carved in the rock lead down into the water. Historians believe that this 'swimming pool' was once used as a fish-tank for the Pollio Felice Villa.

❹ Villa di Pollio Felice★★

Alongside the Bagni are the remains of the Polio Felice Villa. It was built level with the sea, and divided into the *domus* (living quarters) and a separate villa. The villa was large enough for its many rooms and terraces to offer differing views. All along the Sorrento coastline, ancient villas such as this have served as the basis for more modern constructions, with some being converted into hotels.

❺ Divers' sanctuary★

An unusual ceremony takes place every second Sunday in September. In the presence of many small craft, a mass is celebrated on the Vervece rock in honour of the small statue of Mary that lies 12m/40ft below the surface of the waters. As part of the ceremony, flowers are sent down to the statue that watches over 'the people of the sea'. The sculpture is brought ashore to be restored every 10 years.

❻ Marina Grande route★★

This is a pleasant route for a stroll, through both town and countryside, from Sorrento to Marina Grande. Start in Piazza Vittori, where an

attractive white balustrade overlooks the Bay. Follow Via Marina until you reach the old Greek gateway, once the entrance to old Sorrento. A series of staircases leads down to Marina Grande, a small picturesque fishing village much enlivened by numerous bars, restaurants and shops.

❼ O'Parruchiano

Corso Italia, 71/73
☎ **081 878 13 21**
Closed Wed. in low season.

Of the many restaurants in Sorrento, O'Parruchiano ('the parish priest') deserves a special mention. It's here that Enzo Maniello offers the best in traditional Sorrento cuisine. Seated in the shade of orange and lemon trees, you can sample the delights of *gnocchi alla sorrentina*, made with mozzarella and tomatoes, and sprinkled with parmesan, or else try the cannelloni, with a meat,

mozzarella, ricotta and parmesan filling.

❽ Mauro Rinaldi
Via Luigi de Maio, 1/3
☎ **081 807 21 99**
Every day 9am-10pm in summer, 9am-1pm, 4-8pm in low season.

This shop specialises in liqueurs. The most common are lemon-flavoured, such as *liquore di limone* and *crema di limone* (L20,000 a bottle). They also stock *nocino* (walnut), *mandarino* (mandarine), *finocchio* (fennel) and *basilico* (basil) liqueurs in season. A 75cl bottle costs around L16,000. After your return, the liqueurs should be kept in a fridge and served chilled.

Capri, white cliffs and turquoise waters

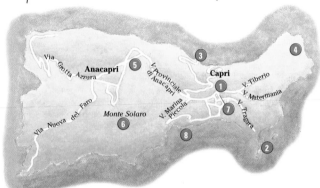

Capri is almost a symbol of Mediterranean beauty, with pink bougainvilleas, green umbrella pines and white cliffs rising steeply out of turquoise waters. No wonder the Emperors Augustus and Tiberius both had residences here. Spring and autumn are the best times of year to visit the island, though you'll still need to keep off the beaten track if you want to avoid the crowds.

❶ The Piazzetta★

A funicular will take you from the Marina Grande port to the Piazzetta ('little square'), the heart of village and island life. The café terraces are busy at all hours, and the square is small enough to be intimate, yet large enough for some discreet celebrity watching as well. The Piazzetta is also the

place from which to set off to go shopping in the luxury boutiques of Via Camerelle, or to go and discover the 'other' island, the lesser-known village of Anacapri.

❷ The Faraglioni★★★

The Faraglioni are three gigantic rocks standing in the sea. The furthest of the three, Scopolo, is said to be the habitat of a famous species of blue lizard that loses its colour if taken off the rock.

For the best view, follow Via Matermania, which also takes you past a huge archway in the rock (the result of natural erosion) and past Villa di Malaparte. The walk can end with a swim in clear, deep waters, amid a landscape that's remained unchanged since Homer's day.

❸ The *Tritone* submarine★
☎ 081 808 66 18
1 Apr.-30 Sep.

The Tritone sets out from Marina Grande to take you on an underwater journey. The descent lasts 40 mins and reaches a depth of 50m/165ft, allowing you to admire all sorts of fish, starfish and corals. A commentary and information about what you see is provided by the crew and ship's computer. The whole trip lasts two hours and costs L50,000.

❹ Villa Jovis★★ ★
Via A. Maiuri
Every day 9am-one hour before sunset.
Entry charge.

Villa Jovis was built for the Emperor Tiberius and dedicated to Jupiter. It has exquisite views of the Sorrento coast. Among the stepped gardens, vast rainwater cisterns, a court area, slaves' quarters, baths and an audience room have been discovered. There's also a spot called 'Tiberius's Drop', from which the Emperor's victims are said to have been flung over 300m/1,000ft into the sea.

❺ Villa San Michele★★★
Anacapri,
Viale A. Munthe, 34
☎ 081 837 14 28
May-Sep. 9am-6pm ,
Oct.-Apr. 10.30am-3.30pm.
Entry charge.

This splendid villa with its own distinctive style bears the traces of the forceful nature of its owner, the Swedish writer and doctor, Axel Munthe. The villa contains a number of interesting archeological artefacts and a truly romantic garden with terraces and pergolas.

❻ Mount Solaro★★
Anacapri
☎ 081 837 14 28
Every day 9am-6pm,
Mar.-Oct. 9.30am-sunset,
Nov.-Feb. 10.30am-3pm
(Wed.-Mon.) Access via a chair-lift (charge).

Mount Solaro (589m/1,932ft) is the highest point on the island. A chair-lift leaving from Anacapri runs you to the top in 12 minutes, whereas it takes one and a half hours on foot. A bar and numerous deckchairs are there to greet you on arrival.

❼ Torta caprese★
It's said that a cook with golden hands first prepared

this cake (whose name means 'Capri cake') for Napoleon's officers during the Russian campaign. Though it may look nothing more than a humble chocolate cake sprinkled with sugar, it is in fact made from the typically Mediterranean mixture of marzipan and South American cocoa. A good place to try some is the Buoncuore patisserie and ice-cream parlour at Vittorio Emanuele, 35 (☎ 081 837 78 26).

❽ Places to swim★★
If you love vast golden sandy beaches, you'll just have to accept that Capri is more a place where you pick your way over the rocks before entering the water. If you really want to sunbathe in the high season, go to bathing establishments, such as La Fontanellina near the Faraglioni, the Lido, and others near Marina Grande. These are usually expensive, and you need to go early or reserve your parasol the day before to be sure of finding what you want.

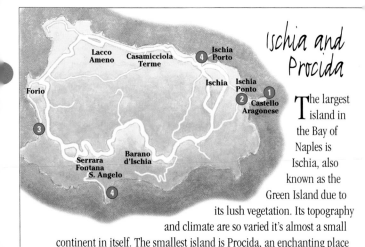

Ischia and Procida

The largest island in the Bay of Naples is Ischia, also known as the Green Island due to its lush vegetation. Its topography and climate are so varied it's almost a small continent in itself. The smallest island is Procida, an enchanting place where life and local traditions have been far less affected by tourism.

❶ Castello Aragonese★★

Ischia Ponte, bus 7 departing from Ischia Porto. Open every day 9am-sunset ☎ 081 99 19 59 Entry charge.

The history of Ischia's rocky offshore islet, on which the castle stands, is the history of the whole island. The fortress, though originally built in 474 BC, only acquired its present-day form during the 14th-16th centuries. Inside this fortified complex is a small city of

buildings added through the ages – the Clarissian convent and its cemetery, the cathedral of the Assunta, as well as several other churches and even a prison.

❷ Calise★★★

Ischia, Via Sogliuzzo, 69 ☎ 081 99 12 70/ 081 198 42 77

The Calise is an excellent bar/patisserie/ice-cream parlour with an impressive array of tasty cakes and ice-creams nestling among a forest of tropical plants. The many delights include *Tortina Bianca*, a cream cake topped with white chocolate, and *Torta al limone*, a cake with a lemon cream filling. The ice-creams are almost large enough to merit a place in the *Guinness Book of Records*.

❸ Poseidon Baths in Ischia★★

Forio, Spiaggia di Citara, bus 1 barred from Ischia Porto ☎ 081 90 71 22 ✆ 081 90 79 95 Every day 8am-7pm. Entry charge.

The volcanic origin of the island has made it an excellent place to take the waters. The Poseidon Baths is a health resort spread over 60,000m²/650,000sqft, with 21 pools – the coldest at 15°C/59°F, the warmest at 40°C/104°F – as well as hydromassage machines, a Jacuzzi and a very hot natural sauna. Remember to book ahead for the mud baths and massages.

❹ A bus tour of Ischia★

There's a bus service that tours the island, and the route is exquisite. It takes around two hours and can be done in two stages. Take the bus (CS) in Ischia Porto and get off at the final stop. From there, a road leads in to Sant'Angelo, a small fishing village, with houses of every colour, situated at the southernmost tip of the island. It's one of the most romantic places on Ischia, and after a rest or a swim there, you'll be ready for the second leg of the trip that takes you back to your starting point.

❺ Architecture in Procida★★★

Typical examples of the architecture of the island can be seen in the ports of Procida and Corricella, with their jumbled rows

of small houses. The buildings with dome-shaped roofs were originally intended as places to store boats in winter, though they've since been modified and enlarged to render them habitable. The façades are usually painted white, pink, red or ochre, and often include arches to

❻ THE GOOD FRIDAY PROCESSION★

Christ's death (*Christo morto*) is remembered every year on Good Friday with a celebratory procession, during which the statue of the dead Christ is carried from the abbey of San Michele through the streets to the island's port. The statue is said to be the work of a crib and figurine artist who was sent to prison for life for committing a terrible crime. However, he received a pardon from the king, after which he sculpted the statue of the dead Christ in token of gratitude. The festival starts at 7am and ends late at night.

decorate the doors, balconies and terraces. Access upstairs is often via an outside staircase.

❼ Terra Murata and the Abbey of San Michele★★

This fortified medieval village dominates the entire island of Procida. Twisting narrow alleyways that rarely see the sun lead up to the 13th-century abbey of San Michele. There's a fine view from the abbey terrace. To visit it, contact the abbot, Don Luigi Fasano (☎ 081 896 76 12), who's always delighted to show visitors around.

The Phlegraean Fields

Cuma
Solfatara
Baia
Pozzuoli
Castello di Baia
Monte Procidia
Bacoli
Bagnoli

This area (whose name derives from the Greek word meaning 'burning') owes its reputation as much to its rich history and myths as to its volcanic activity. The landscape is fascinating, as are the traces of its fiery past – dormant craters, lava flows and engulfed cities, which, together with its beaches, are all to be found in the relatively enclosed area around the Bay of Pozzuoli.

❶ Pozzuoli★

Pozzuoli means 'little wells', a reminder of the region's underground thermal activity. In the 2nd century BC, 'Puteoli' was one of the most thriving Roman settlements. The amphitheatre survives from this golden age. The historic town centre (called the Rione Terra, and still undergoing restoration) was evacuated in 1971 after earth movements known as bradyseisms, which still condition life in Pozzuoli today.

❷ Solfatara★★

Via Solfatara, 161
☎ **081 526 23 41**
Every day 8.30am-one hour before sunset.
Entry charge.

The Solfatara is a 700m/2,300ft-wide crater created by an explosion 4,000 years ago. Strange volcanic phenomena – the ever-present smell of sulphurous gas continuously bubbling up to the surface and the greenish tinge of sulphur deposits on the rocks – make it appear even more mysterious.

❸ Oasi Naturalistica di Monte Nuovo★

Via Virgilio, Arco Felice Pozzuoli
☎ **081 526 76 49**
Every day 9am-one hour before sunset.

The Monte Nuovo, or 'New Mount', is so called because it's the youngest in Europe and was formed as recently as 1538 as the result of an eruption. As the area isn't high (140m/460ft) and is protected from the wind, it's pleasant for walking. There are three routes (lasting one, two or three hours), all of which allow you to see the geological and botanical

features at first hand. There's also an excellent view of the Bay of Pozzuoli. For guided tours, contact the Centro Studi dell'Oasi.

❹ Baia Castle and Archaeological Museum★★
Via Castello, à Baia
☎ 081 523 37 97
Every day 9am-one hour before sunset.
Entry charge.

The Aragonese fortress, built on a steep promontory above the sea, was begun in 1495, and only recently became the site of the Archaeological Museum of the Phlegraean Fields. One of the towers houses the chapel dedicated to the cult of the Emperor, reconstructed after its removal from the forum of Miseno that is now partly under water. Baia also has some good spots for bathing.

❺ Stufe di Nerone★★
Via Stufe di Nerone, 37, Baia
☎ 081 868 80 06.

These thermal baths offer you the chance to swim in a warm open-air pool, slip into a cavity in the rocks for a sauna or simply relax as you listen to whoever's chatting behind the nearest cloud of steam. The waters here are rich in bromium and iodine, which means they're invigorating, anti-inflammatory and good for relieving rheumatism. You'll find plenty to do here.

❻ Casina Vanvitelliana★★★
Via Fusaro à Bacoli
Every day 9am-one hour before sunset.

This so-called 'small house', delicately designed by Vanvitelli in 1782 and then forgotten until its restoration in 1991, is set in the romantic location (the silhouette of the house is reflected on the surface of Lake Fusano) that witnessed the love affair between King Ferdinand IV of Bourbon and his second wife, Lucia Migliaccio. The Casina may also have inspired Mozart and Rossini, who were both guests here – who knows?

❼ Il Casolare★★
Contrada Coste dei Fondi di Bahia, Bacoli
☎ 081 523 51 93. Cl. Mon.

This small restaurant is in a fascinating location alongside a crater. The menu is more than plentiful – a selection of starters, two *primi*, a meat dish served with vegetables, homemade dessert and a chestnut or chocolate liqueur for just L.39,000. All the ingredients, including the wine, come from the Casolare. The cooking is always of a high standard (sometimes there are themed meals, i.e. meals based on cheese or wild boar, etc.), and it's also possible to sleep here at weekends.

❽ THE ARCHEOLOGICAL PARK IN CUMAE★★★
Via Acropoli, à Cuma
☎ 081 854 30 60
Every day 9am-one hour before sunset.
Entry charge.

Cumae is the oldest of the Greek colonies in what is today Western Europe. Excavation of the site has not yet been completed. Among the archeological riches already found, the most exciting is the Cave of Sibyl, at the foot of the Acropolis. This is a 130m/427ft-long trapezoid gallery that captures strange light effects due to niches carved in the walls. According to legend, this is where the Sibyl, who read the oracles, predicted Aeneas's fate to him. Unfortunately, the truth is likely to be more prosaic, and it was in all probability a military installation.

Rooms and restaurants Practicalities

HOTELS

A ROOM WITH A VIEW

Location and price are the two key factors in choosing a hotel. If you think you'll enjoy lively Neapolitan street life, choose somewhere in the historic or civic centre. For a room with a view of the Bay of Naples, pick a hotel higher up on the hill (in Corso Vittorio Emmanuele or Posillipo). As a compromise, you could stay in one of the luxury seafront hotels opposite the Castel dell'Ovo. They're centrally located and have a view of Vesuvius. If you're very lucky, you may have a view of Capri as well. Prices are high, but not ridiculously so. When you book your room, remember to ask for a view of the Bay of Naples. Some (though not all) hotels charge a supplement for the view, though it's not excessive. It's worth checking when you book.

OFFICIAL CATEGORIES AND TARIFS

There are five official categories of hotels, rated from 1 to 5 stars. As a rule, prices are high. It's rare to find a room for much less than L100,000, and even then the decor is unlikely to be very original. A room in a comfortable hotel will cost L150,000-200,000.

Prices are required to be displayed inside rooms but can vary according to the time of year. On arrival, you'll be asked for your passport, as hotels in Italy are legally obliged to fill in a registration form.

RESERVING FROM HOME

It's quite customary to make a telephone reservation (English is usually spoken) before you arrive in Naples. You may be asked to send a deposit, which you can pay by international money order or by sending a fax giving your credit card number and its expiry date, and confirming the dates of your stay, what rooms you want (single, twin or, if you want a double bed, *matrimoniale*), and the number of guests. Hotels in Naples usually expect you to reserve a month or two in advance, but if you plan to visit in May,

book well ahead because 'Monuments in May' attracts many visitors. If you plan to come during the high season and want to stay in a reasonably-priced hotel on the islands or along the Amalfi or Sorrento coast during the high season, you should reserve 4-6 months in advance. If you have a car, some hotels have car parking facilities. If you find it hard to sleep when it's very hot, request a room with air-conditioning, and make sure it doesn't overlook a tiny inner courtyard or one of the city's busiest streets. Prices quoted are usually for a double room, and any further guests will pay extra. Breakfast may be included in the price, but it's important to check.

RESTAURANTS

OPENING HOURS AND MEALTIMES

Mealtimes are typical of a Mediterranean city. Neapolitans sit down to eat later than many other nations: lunch starts at around 1.30-2pm and dinner 9.00-9.30pm. However, mealtimes are often flexible and it isn't difficult to find somewhere to eat at more unorthodox hours. To avoid a lengthy wait, arrive half an hour before peak times, especially on Friday and Saturday evenings or public holidays. You can always reserve a table in a smart restaurant, though it isn't normally possible in the more informal *trattorie* and pizzerias. Many restaurants close on Sundays.

PRICES

Service isn't included in the prices, and so appears as a separate charge based on the total of your bill. Expect also to pay a cover charge of L2,000-4,000 per person. Tips are always welcome. The choice of restaurants is wide, and prices are reasonable – much more so than in hotels. You can pay as little as L10,000 per person for a pizza and drink, or eat a meal for around L30,000 in a family-run *trattoria* offering simple but tasty traditional dishes. Restaurants are generally smarter than *trattorie* and meals start at around L50,000.

FAST FOOD

If you feel like a snack between meals, there's plenty to choose from in the way of Italian-style fast food – which has been able to resist the encroachment of the McDonalds of the world. In pizzerias you'll find *pizzette*

('little pizzas'), as well as pizza folded in two, and delicious *saltimbocche* (literally, 'jump in your mouth') – a kind of sandwich made from pizza dough with a range of fillings (such as mushroom, ham, aubergine or cheese). Otherwise, go to a small grocery store (*salumeria*) where they'll make you a fresh *panino* (sandwich). Snacks are delicious and never expensive.

AN ITALIAN MEAL

A proper Italian meal consists of an *antipasto* (starter), a *primo* (a first course of either pasta or a *risotto*), a *secondo* (meat or fish) with *contorni* (vegetables) that are ordered separately, a dessert (*frutta*, or *dolce*, i.e. a sweet) and coffee, concluding with a liqueur (for example, a *limoncello* or *amaro*). Neapolitan cooking is often highly salted.

It isn't sensible to sit down to eat in a smart restaurant if all you want is a bowl of pasta, and it isn't worth paying the extra price.

Trattorie often serve local wines in jugs. White wines are particularly good, and some will be sparkling (*frizzante*). For further details about local wines, check the shopping section (pp.110-111). Mineral water is either still (*liscia*) or sparkling (*gassata*), and Italian beers go as well as wine with a pizza or light meal – try Nastro Azzurro or Peroni, or a local beer on tap.

UNMISSABLE SPECIALITIES

As well as the dishes mentioned in the culinary calendar on p.22, there are other well-known specialities. *Spaghetti alle vongole in bianco* is a sauce of clams with white wine. '*In rosso*', the clams are in tomato sauce. Lots of other pasta dishes are prepared with a seafood sauce.

Gnocchi alla sorrentina are potato noodles served in a tomato and mozzarella sauce.

Friarelli are a kind of green vegetables that grow only in Campania. Its unusual taste goes well with sausages.

Calamari (squid, fried just enough to be crunchy), and octopus are served with a salad or sauce.

Fish are grilled or boiled in *acqua pazza* (literally, 'mad water').

Marinated anchovies (slightly spicy) are eaten as a starter. Stuffed vegetables (*ripieni*) include peppers.

HOTELS

Santa Lucia, Lungomare

Excelsior ★★★★★
Via Partenope, 48
☎ 081 764 01 11
𝐅 081 764 97 43
From L420,000 (without

view) to L470,000 (with view, including breakfast).

The monumental entrance provides a taste of what to expect inside, a luxurious Belle Epoque setting of mirrors, marble, columns and chandeliers. Many famous guests have stayed at the Excelsior. The elegant rooms are traditionally furnished and decorated, and overlook one of the most beautiful panoramas in the world.

Grande Albergo Vesuvio ★★★★
Via Partenope, 45
☎ 081 764 00 44

𝐅 081 764 44 83
L400,000-470,000.

Built in 1882 by a Belgian baron, the Vesuvio is the oldest seafront hotel. The famous Caruso suite, where the great Neapolitan tenor spent his last night, still contains his piano.

The halls named after Scarlatti and Puccini are delightful. Recently refurbished, the

Vesuvio is the place to come to if you want comfort and un-rivalled views of the Bay of Naples.

Miramare ★★★★
Via N. Sauro, 24
☎ 081 764 75 89
𝐅 081 764 07 75
L300,000-390,000 (with view).

If you prefer your luxury with a more human touch, you're sure to appreciate the warm welcome at the Miramare, managed by Enzo and Bibi Rosolino. Built at the turn of the century, this aristocratic villa has retained its Liberty furnishings and tasteful decor. In summer, breakfast is served on the terrace, from which you can see Vesuvius. The Miramare also provides its guest with bicycles for trips around Naples.

Hotel Rex★★

Via Palepoli, 12
☎ 081 764 93 89
📠 081 764 92 27
L170,000 (including breakfast).

If you particularly want to stay near the seafront but are willing to forego a view of the Bay of Naples, then try the Rex, which offers rooms at sensible prices. The rooms are comfortable, if a little unimaginatively furnished.

Le Fontane del Mare★

Via N. Tommaseo, 14
☎ 081 764 38 11
📠 081 764 34 70

From L114 000 (with view, without bath) to L144 000 (with bath, but without view, including breakfast).

This small, friendly *pensione* has no great pretensions. It's ideal for anyone who expects to spend very little time in the hotel during the day and isn't looking for luxury. The building retains its original interior. The rooms with a view are former drawing rooms and have no bathrooms, and the rooms with bathrooms have no view. It's your choice.

Panoramic views

Britannique★★★★

Corso V. Emmanuele, 133
☎ 081 761 41 45
📠 081 66 04 67
L220,000-250,000 (with view and breakfast).

The Britannique is a household name in Naples. Its rooms are full of light and tastefully decorated. There's a fine view of the Bay of Naples and an attractive garden with lush Mediterranean vegetation, away from the bustle of the city centre. A private staircase leads directly up to Piazza Amedeo, in the more exclusive part of the city.

Grand Hotel Parker's★★★★

Corso V. Emmanuele, 135
☎ 081 761 24 74
📠 081 66 35 27
L280,000-340,000 (including breakfast).

Here you 'll find a blend of late 19th-century elegance and sumptuous modern-day comfort. Parker's, renovated in 1990, has lost none of its old-world atmosphere, and still has lounges with period furniture and valuable oil paintings. There are two restaurants, and in one you'll be able to try recipes dating back to the Bourbon era. There's also a view of Capri.

Chiaia and San Pasquale

Majestic★★★★

Largo Vasto a Chiaia, 68
☎ 081 41 65 00
📠 081 41 01 45
L270,000 (with or without view, including breakfast).

The Majestic is in a smart district, and is therefore well situated for shoppers. In fact, the temptations start as soon as you set foot outside the hotel. Along with the Excelsior and Vesuvio, the Majestic is part of the Prestige Hotel chain. It's the least expensive and most modern of the three. All rooms above the 6th floor have a marvellous view.

Pinto Storey★★★

Via G. Martucci, 72
☎ 081 68 12 60
📠 081 66 75 36
L125,000-185,000.

This is a delightful hotel perched on the 4th and 5th floors of an elegant building in Via Martucci (and if you're lucky, you'll be given a room with a view). The Pinto Storey was started in 1868, and owes its origins and name to Signora Pinto and Mr Storey who fell in love, married and ran the business together. It has an attractive wood-panelled decor, and is conveniently located for both visits and shopping.

Mergellina and Pausillipe

Paradiso★★★

Via Catullo, 11
☎ 081 761 41 61
🖷 081 761 34 49
L280,000
(with or without view, including breakfast).

The Paradiso is on the Posillipo hillside, overlooking the sea below. It's away from the noisiest parts of Naples, though still conveniently located, with the nearby funicular railway leading down to the small port of Mergellina. The style of the hotel is perhaps a little over-romantic for some, but the view from the terrace is breath-taking, and it's a paradise for honeymooners.

Splendid★★★

Via Manzoni, 96
☎ and 🖷 081 64 54 62
L195 000-200,000
(including breakfast).

Located in a quiet street in a residential part of Naples, the Splendid offers something rare in Naples – tranquillity! All *matrimoniale* rooms (those with double beds) have a superb view of the coast road leading through the Phlegraean Fields. Car parking facilities are available.

Canada ★★★

Via Mergellina, 43
☎ and 🖷 081 68 09 52
L160,000-260,000
(with view).

The basic, functional decor at the Canada is livened up with colourful paintings and flourishing plants. The rooms are all named after flowers, and are comfortable and cheery, and some enjoy a sea view. Perhaps best of all, the Canada is right by the port of Mergellina, the embarkation point for all hydrofoil services to the islands.

Ausonia★★

Via Caracciolo, 11
☎ 081 66 45 36
🖷 081 68 22 78
L160,000
(including breakfast).

You might think a seafront hotel with an anchor as its symbol is not the place for you. Yet you don't need to be an old sea dog to enjoy the calm 'marine' decor of this charming hotel. So just book a room with a view, and you'll soon feel like a fish in water.

Historic city centre

Hotel Duomo★

Via Duomo, 228
☎ and 🖷 081 26 59 88
L100,000
(with bathroom).

The Duomo is housed on the first floor of a 19th-century building, and is easy enough to miss. However, it's worth noting for its excellent prices. Moreover, although it's located in the heart of Naples, the Duomo offers quiet, spacious rooms.

Albergo Sansevero★

Via S. M. Costantinopoli, 101
☎ 081 21 09 07
🖷 081 21 16 98
L140,000
(including breakfast).

This hotel is run by the same management but is located on Piazza Bellini. It opened recently, and is a pleasant place to stay, though the decor is sometimes a little sparse. The rooms are large and all have en-suite bathrooms. If you ask for a voucher, you can have a real Neapolitan breakfast with *sfogliatelle* at the next-door café.

A word of advice – if you want a quiet stay, ask for a room overlooking the courtyard.

Soggiorno Sansevero

**Piazza S. Domenico Maggiore, 9 /
Via Costantinopoli
☎ 081 551 59 49
☏ 081 21 16 98
L80,000-90,000 (without bathroom), L110,000-130,000 (with bathroom).**

This is the ideal place if you love old *palazzi*. Run by Signora Arminda, this *pensione* is housed inside what was once the residence of Prince Sansevero. While the rooms themselves may not be princely, they do at least look out onto the courtyard and are quiet. This is not to be undervalued, as the very beautiful Piazza San Domenico is lively far into the night.

Hotel Europeo★★

**Via Mezzocanone,109C
☎ 081 551 72 54
☏ 081 552 22 62
L70,000-120,000-
(with bathroom).**

The Hotel Europeo is in fact a *pensione* located in the heart of Naples' Latin Quarter. It's an unpretentious establishment, housed on the third floor, and popular with university students, night-owls and those who enjoy dreaming above the rooftops of the city. Furnishings are basic and functional. Be sure to ask for a room with a bathroom, as not all the rooms have one.

Hotel Suite Esedra★★★

**Via Cantani, 12
☎ and ☏ 081 553 70 87/
081 28 74 51
L185,000 (incl. breakfast).**

The Esedra is a real treat. It has 15 artfully-decorated rooms, each dedicated to a sign of the zodiac. The rooms have balconies with flowers and bathrooms with majolica fittings, as well as linen curtains to make you feel at home. Since being restored, this *palazzo* in the heart of Naples has a swimming pool and jacuzzi in a hanging garden. The Esedra is a 4-star hotel at 3-star prices, and the staff will make you feel welcome.

Historic and civic centre

Jolly Hotel★★★★

**Via Medina, 70
☎ 081 41 60 00
☏ 081 551 80 10
L245 000-290,000.**

The Jolly Hotel would be difficult to miss – it's the only skyscraper in the centre of Naples. It has 30 floors, and was built in the 1950s, since when it's become a regular conference venue. It's popular with businessmen and other guests for its central location and its restaurant with a 360° view of the city. The best views are to be had from the 16th floor upwards.

Toledo★★★

**Via Montecalvario, 15
☎ and ☏ 081 40 68 00
L120,000-160,000
(including breakfast).**

If you like contrasts, the Toledo is for you. The building, weathered by time, blends in perfectly with its surroundings, one of Naples' oldest working-class districts. The inside of the hotel, however, has undergone a complete renovation. The rooms are comfortable and functional, and there's a pleasant bar, as well as a hidden gem in the form of a terrace garden with a splendid view of the Castel Sant'Angelo.

Executive Hotel★★★

**Via del Cerriglio, 10
☎ and ☏ 081 552 06 11
and 081 552 39 80
L200,000-270,000.**

Though by no means located in Naples' most attractive street, the hotel is right in the heart of the business centre, and only five minutes from the historic centre and the departure point for the islands. Despite its rather austere exterior, it has bright, pleasant rooms. You can start the day with breakfast on the terrace looking out over the rooftops, and finish the day in the sauna relaxing after all your sightseeing.

RESTAURANTS

PRICES

The following classification takes the price of meals into account.:

★★★★: L75,000-100,000
★★★: L55,000-75,000
★★: L30,000-55,000
★: under L30,000

The heart of the old city

A Canzuncella★★★

Piazza S. Maria la Nova, 18
☎ 081 551 90 18
Closed Sun. evening.

A Canzunella ('little song') has the perfect combination of good food and music. Every Saturday night for the past 45 years, Aurelio has been donning his straw hat and singing on the small stage in the middle of the room. The entire restaurant is dedicated to music, to the old Neapolitan songs and to parody. It's an ideal way to end the evening after sampling Marisa's excellent cooking.

Ciro a Santa Brigida★★★

Via Santa Brigida, 71
☎ 081 552 40 72
Closed Sun.

Although the decor may be nothing out of the ordinary, the mozzarella and the fish soup certainly are. Antonio Pace, the owner, is also president of the Association of Neapolitan Restaurateurs. Apart from making an excellent pizza, the chef (one of the best-known in the area) also prepares a memorable bean soup with chestnuts, as well as a delicious *sartù di riso*, a traditional local dish consisting of a timbale of rice garnished with peas, meat, mozzarella and meat sauce.

Il Cucciolo Bohemien★★

Vico Berio, 5/8
☎ 081 40 79 02
Closed Sun.

The walls of this restaurant tell a story, part of the story of Naples. The owners jokingly call them the wailing walls. The first room has its walls covered in cartoons depicting the Naples football team's hours of glory and disappointment. The second is lined with signed photos of San Carlo artists. An interesting decor for a typically Neapolitan meal in a very friendly atmosphere.

Pizzeria Brandi★

Salita Sant'Anna di Palazzo, 1
☎ 081 41 69 28
Closed Mon.

Right by Via Chiaia is the pizzeria owned by Eduardo Pagnani. It's been famous throughout the world since 1889, the year the margherita pizza was invented here in honour of Margaret of Savoy. The stone plaque by the door recalls the event, as does the house slogan 'Where the pizza is a piece of history'. But nowadays the historic margherita pizza is just as renowned here for the thinness of its crust and timed-to-perfection cooking. It's no surprise to learn many illustrious clients have come through the doors – from Luciano Pavarotti and Gerard Depardieu to Chelsea Clinton. It's difficult to get seated at the small table opposite the balcony or at one of the two tables outside, but you could always try reserving the day before.

Santa Lucia / Borgo marinaro

La Cantinella★★★★

Via Cuma, 42
☎ 081 764 86 84
Closed Sun. May-Sep.

From La Cantinella's veranda, in one of the most attractive settings in the city centre, you could once admire Vesuvius rising up over the Bay of Naples. Until 1996, that is, when the local authorities ordered its removal. But there's still a wonderful view and many of La Cantinella's attractions are to be found in the kitchen. You could try the *linguine alla Santa Lucia* (fresh pasta with tomato sauce, octopus, cuttlefish, shrimps and seafood). La Cantinella also has

one of the best wine cellars in Naples. You can visit it, and buy wine with the help of the maitre d'.

Da Ettore★

Via S. Lucia, 56
☎ 081 764 04 98
Closed Sun.

This pizzeria has been open for over a century and used to be a shop selling 'wines and cooking', such as you still find in some parts of Naples. Nowadays Da Ettore is one of the best 'ovens' around. An absolute must is the *pagnotiello*, an enormous turnover of baked pasta dough with the filling of your choice (it's delicious with parma ham and mozzarella) that can be ordered to take away. A terrace is set up in summer. The service is always very good, and since the restaurant is always packed, try to reserve in advance.

La Bersagliera★★★

Borgo Marinaro
☎ 081 764 60 16
Closed Tue.

Inside the fishing port and right in the heart of the beautiful Borgo Marinaro area, La Bersagliera's terrace looks out to sea. The cooking here is traditional Neapolitan with a predominance of fish and seafood dishes, all to be eaten to the tapping of masts in the background and the smells of the sea all around you. It's a romantic setting, especially if you ignore the over-bright neon sign. Your predecessors at the tables of this establishment include Salvador Dali, Sophia Loren, Totò and Marcello Mastroianni.

Riviera

Da Dora ★★★★

Via F. Palasciano, 30
☎ 081 68 05 19
Closed Sun.

Da Dora is the restaurant in which to eat fish in Naples. You'll find it in an alleyway leading down to the Riviera di Chiaia. It's frequented by the cream of Neapolitan society, and serves first-rate food in an atmosphere that has remained intimate and friendly. Dora is the cook, and her sons are fishermen – so there's no need

to worry about the freshness of the ingredients (one of the reasons the restaurant is so famous). As a *primo*, try either the *tagliatelle ai ricci* (with sea urchins) or *linguine alla Dora* (with a sauce including lobster, prawns, scampi and squid).

Vadinchenia ★★

Via Pontano, 21
☎ 081 66 19 58/
081 66 01 17
Closed Sun. and Mon.

The cuisine here is both original and imaginative, though still very Mediterranean. You eat at widely-spaced tables (unusual for Naples), in a grey and white decor designed by Philippe Starck. The regional recipes, carefully prepared by the chef, come with a selection of wines to match a style of cuisine that's slightly different from the purely Neapolitan. It's also worth visiting the wine-tasting section in the basement.

Da Tonino★

Via S. Teresa a Chiaia, 47
☎ 081 42 15 33
Closed Sun.

The owner (a man with a self-deprecating sense of humour) says of his *trattoria* (one of the oldest in Naples) that it's a place with character, and that his clientele either have to put up with it or go elsewhere. Indeed, the scenes between Nina, the cook, and Antonio, her husband who serves the food, are legendary. 'Here we do everything with laughter and love… though it may not always seem so,' they say. Da Tonino is a place where you can order the day's special in complete confidence. You're sure to find wonderful cuisine, good service and a human touch, all at a reasonable price.

Mergellina and Posilippo

La Sacrestia★★★

Via Orazio, 116
☎ 081 761 10 51
Closed Mon.(low season) or Sun. (summer).

This is one of the best restaurants in Naples. It's housed in an old villa, and the decor (based on a real sacristy) was the idea of filmmaker Flavio Moreghini. The terrace has a splendid view of the Bay of Naples, and in summer is always in full bloom. The sophisticated fish-based cuisine combines traditional dishes with the latest gastronomic inventions. The Sacrestia is a definite must – as long as you're not worried about prices.

Rosiello★★★

Via S.Strato, 10
☎ 081 769 12 88
Closed Wed.

In this restaurant the recipes are handed down through the family. The view, like that in many a picture postcard, combines Vesuvius and the Mediterranean, and the menu has both land and sea dishes. To sample the land dishes, try the courgette (zucchini) and courgette flower soup. For the sea dishes, go for the *linguine con cicalla di mare* (the now rare sea cicada). The Rosiello is also known for its traditional Neapolitan patisseries (*babà* and *pastiera*) and more *casareccia* (homemade) examples, such as tarts made with homemade jam.

Al Poeta★★

Piazza S. di Giacomo, 133
☎ 081 575 69 36
Closed Mon.

You'll feel at home here. Fish in all manner of very delicious guises – grilled, or cooked in *acqua pazza*, i.e. tomato sauce – is on offer, along with a wide choice of wines. Indeed, 300 different wines are available, making this one of the best-stocked cellars in Naples. It's also one of the few restaurants in Posilippo not to have a view of the Bay – a small matter, since the three Neapolitan chefs draw the clientele with an imaginative cuisine, particularly when it comes to *primi*. Among others, try the *spaghetti con ciccinielli* (with minnows).

Vini e Cucina★

Corso V. Emmanuele, 762
☎ 081 66 03 02
Closed Mon.

Located opposite the pretty station of Mergellina, this unremarkable quiet *trattoria* serves traditional dishes in a sober setting. Its tasty daily specials are based on wholesome family recipes handed down from the 1950s, when the restaurant first opened. The food is good and the prices as modest as the decor.

Ciro a Mergellina★★★

Via Mergellina, 17-21
☎ 081 68 17 80
Closed Mon.

Ciro is one of the best spots for Neapolitan cuisine. It serves really good *antipasti*, seafood, fish, pasta and pizzas, and has a spacious terrace from which to see and be seen. Unfortunately, it's often crowded, especially in the high season, and therefore can be noisy. You almost always have to book in summer.

Spaccanapoli and Portalba

Symposium★★★

Via B. Croce, 38
☎ 081 551 85 10
Open Fri. and Sat.

If you're looking for an opportunity to try medieval and Renaissance cuisine, come to the Symposium. Its mission is to recreate Italian dishes from the Middle Ages through to 1915, and serve them on theme nights. The banquets are a chance to discover dishes and decors from the past and take in a show. A single table is set for 20 people, and Giovanni explains the secrets of the recipes and tells you about the etiquette of the day. The show depends on the period, and could include music, poetry and sketches. Reservations need to be made by the previous Tuesday at the latest, and the set meal costs L70,000.

Lombardi a Santa Chiara★★

Via B. Croce, 59
☎ 081 552 07 80
Closed Mon.

A few steps away from the church in Santa Chiara, the Lombardi family (who also have a restaurant in Porta S. Gennaro) are known for their pizzas cooked in

a wood-fired oven. Among the many dishes on offer, why not try the house speciality – *pizza alla Lombardi* (smoked *provola* cheese, goat's cheese, tomatoes and basil). Though housed on three different levels, including the basement, the restaurant is often full, and is probably best avoided on Saturday evenings. It's a nice place to come from autumn to spring, but is often too hot in summer.

Per Scoprire
il Mondo della
Cucina Araba.
Shish Kebab
Cous Cous
Hommos e Falafel
Tabbuleh
Maqluba

La Taverna dell' Arte★★

Rampe S. Giovanni
Maggiore, 1 A
☎ 081 552 75 58
Closed Sun.

Located a little away from the bustle of Naples, though still easy to find, the Taverna is a mix of charm, elegance and tradition. Its motto is 'real cooking – not just for tourists'. It combines elements of aristocratic dishes with more popular fare. The onion soufflé and the cod with black olives, tomatoes, pine kernels and dried raisins are both excellent,

as are the basil sorbet and the blancmange. Tables are set out under the pergola in summer. It's best to reserve.

Kebab Express★

Via Sedile del Porto, 71
☎ 081 552 91 04
Closed Sun. lunchtiime.

This restaurant was opened a couple of years ago by Omar, right in the heart of the university district (and is an offshoot of the Hassultan Bar). The room is small but always very welcoming – not least thanks to the smiles of Omar and the talent of the chefs. You'll find many Lebanese, Syrian and Iranian specialities, among them a kind of rice timbale called *makluba* (rice, chicken and aubergine) and *qôsi*, as well as hot and cold starters. All in all, an opportunity for a delicious and exotic respite from the ever-present pasta.

Via Tribunali

Di Matteo★

Via Tribunali, 94
☎ 081 29 42 03
Closed Sun.

This pizzeria became famous during the 1994 G7 summit on the day Bill Clinton unexpectedly turned up to eat here. Before then, it was already well-known – now it's an institution. This has its drawbacks, as on Saturday nights the wait for a table can be lengthy, and the pizzas are not always as perfectly cooked as they might be. Nevertheless, the service is efficient. Outside you can buy delicious snacks, including mini-pizzas and fried specialities, such as

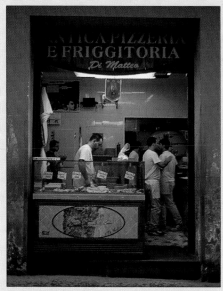

arancini, crocche, aubergine (eggplant) fritters and courgette (zucchini) flower fritters in season.

Bellini★★
Via S. Maria di Costantinopoli, 80
☎ 081 45 97 74
Closed Sun.

The Bellini has three great specialities: *linguine al cartoccio* (cooked in foil with a seafood sauce), *pizza Bellini* (ham, mushrooms and mozzarella) and the waiters! They're so moody and constantly unpredictable they've become part of the restaurant's reputation. The *risotto terra e mare* is also very good. But avoid the house white wine. The Bellini has a largish terrace in summer.

La Campagnola★
Via dei Tribunali, 47
☎ 081 45 90 34
Closed evenings and Sun.

The sign outside the door states, 'Eat well and spend little.' And you will, even if the prices have increased in line with this tiny restaurant's reputation. The first room has a display of the many wines from the cellar, and you can try glasses of the wines of the day before sitting down for your meal. The menu is written on a slate, and is gradually erased as dishes run out. The Campagnola has a family atmosphere, and offers the simple old-fashioned charm associated with plastic red-and-white checked tablecloths.

Da Carmine★
Via dei Tribunali, 330
☎ 081 29 43 83
Closed Sun.

The decor here is a little bare, though it won't stop Don Carmine simmering his exquisite *capretto* (kid) with potatoes in the kitchen. The other members of his family serve the food and insult each other, all under the loud orders of Adele. The dishes are simple and tasty. Apart from *capretto*, there are *gnocchi alla sorrentina,* and all the fresh pasta is good. The *trattoria* also opens at lunchtime on Sunday during the Christmas period and 'Monuments in May' season.

Cantina di Via Sapienza★
Via Sapienza, 40/41
☎ 081 45 90 78/
081 29 09 83
Open lunchtime only, cl. Sun.

This is an old *'vini e cucina'* cellar dating back to the turn of the century. There are few tables, and the atmosphere is intimate. You can buy wine here, the food is good and the prices are reasonable (L18,000 including wine, service and cover charge). They have a choice of simple regional dishes – *friarelli,* cod and *pasta e fagioli,* and tasty soups – *zuppa di carne cotta* (cooked meats), *zuppa di soffritto* (with pig's entrails), and the famous Neapolitan *ragù*.

Duomo and station

Mimi alla Ferrovia★★★
Via A. d'Aragona, 21
☎ 081 553 85 25
Closed Sun.

Since it's near the law courts, this is a favourite haunt of lawyers, which is not to say that it hasn't also been visited by stars of the stage and screen, such as Fellini and Totò. This recently-renovated 'temple of Neapolitan cooking' is renowned for its endless array of starters (40 at the last count), and for the quality and excellent preparation of the fish dishes (either baked in tin foil, in the oven, with salt, or in *acqua pazza*). Another speciality is, of course, the *linguine alla Mimi*, made with Mediterranean prawns, scampi and

other seafood. You can also try Le Lettere, the homemade house white wine.

Da Michele★
Via C. Sersale, 1
☎ 081 553 92 04
Closed Sun.

Here you'll find the definitive pizza, at its most straightforward and exquisite. Only two types are served – the margherita and the marinara (with garlic, olive oil, tomatoes and oregano), which was invented here by Michele Condurro, the grandfather of the present owner. Da Michele has been open since 1888, and the place has changed little since the 1930s. It comprises two rooms round a central wood-fired oven. You won't find the same level of price and quality elsewhere (L7,000 for a pizza and beer). The place is always full.

Trianon Pizzeria★
Via P. Colletta, 42/46
☎ 081 553 94 26
Cl. Sun. lunch.

The Trianon is one of the most popular pizzerias in Naples. The upstairs room is the best, and is decorated with stucco and mirrors. The menu lists 15 or so pizzas, but the chef will make up anything you ask for. All you have to do is select the pizza you want and the size you want it – mini, normal or maxi.

Vomero

Il Cortile★★
Viale A. Allbini, 3 A
☎ 081 560 40 48
Closed Mon.

Il Cortile resembles the paved inner courtyard and garden of an apartment building. Around you are small shops. You can choose your pasta dish from the 'grocery' corner, and the wine for your meal from the 'café-bar' corner. The atmosphere is convivial and ideal for trying out the light, creative cuisine of Giancarlo Galasso. The menu changes every day, but two things are always recommended – the homemade bread (delicious, and with olives) and the dishes with squash (that goes so well with *gnocchi*). The lasagne with green vegetables and the *raviolini alla caprese* are also well worth trying. The *panna cotta* is delicious for dessert.

Orto
Botanico

PZA L.
PODERICO

Corso

Foria

Corso Malta

Via N.va
Poggioreale

V. Arenaccia

PIAZZA
NAZIONALE

Via

Via

Casanova

C.so Novara

Corso
Meridionale

Garibaldi

PIAZZA
CAPUANA

Via Carbonara

**Museo
Archeologico
Nazion.**

Via S. Teresa di Scalzi

PIAZZA CAVOUR

Via E. Pessina

V. Firenze

**Staz.
Centrale**

**S. Maria
Donnaregina**

V. Poerio

PIAZZA

Duomo

GARIBALDI

Via

del

Tribunali

V. Vicaria
Vecchia

Via P. Colletta

Corso A. Lucci

**S. Lorenzo
Maggiore**

Via G.
Ferraris

Corso

Via

**S. Domenico
Maggiore**

Via S. Biagio
ai Librai

Corso

Garibaldi

PZA
DANTE

Via B. Croce

V. Anna
Lombo

Via Roma

**Palazzo
Cuomo**

PZA N.
AMORE

Duomo

Via P. Umberto

Via A. Vespucci

S. Chiara

PZA DEL
MERCATO

Via Marinella

**Pal.
Gravina**

Corso

Via A.

V. Toledo

M.te Oliveto

Marina

PZA
CARITÀ

Via

Sanfelice

PZA
BOVIA

Via Nuova

Via A. Diaz

Via A. Depretis

V. de Gasperi

V. C. Colombo

Via Medina

Bacino del Piliero

**PIAZZA
MUNICIPIO**

Via S. Carlo

Staz.

**Castel
Nuovo**

F. Acton

**Palazzo
Reale**

PIAZZA
PLEBISCITO

Via

Via C. Console

Porto Beverello

Via Santa Luccia

Via N. Sauro

Via Toledo

**Castel
Il'Ovo**

| 0 | 200 | 400 m |

| 0 | 200 | 400 yds |

● **Where to shop**

● **Nightlife**

Shopping Practicalities

There are two different ways to shop in Naples: you can either indulge in smart window-shopping in expensive boutiques, following the weekend shopping routes taken by Neapolitans, or else wander at leisure through the old alleyways of the historic city centre in search of more unusual items, perhaps in the craft shops that are typical of the city.

WHERE TO SHOP

Certain districts of Naples are more specialised than others. For designer clothes, you'll find the luxury boutiques in and around Piazza dei Martiri. The area around Via dei Mille is still fairly smart. Alternatively, there's Via Chiaia, which offers more informal styles. The Vomero district has numerous clothes, shoe and accessory shops. Via Toledo has attractive shops in the pedestrian area near the Palazzo Reale, but shops in the upper part of Via Toledo, such as Corso Umberto, tend to be rather scruffy. If you're looking for furniture or fittings, there are numerous shops around Piazza Municipio and Via dei Mille. For antiques, head for Via D. Morelli, or towards Via Constantinopoli in the historic centre.

CRAFTS

Crafts are to be found in the historic centre, and the craftsmen are still located by trade, as in the old days.

Via S. Gregorio Armeno
Neapolitan cribs and figurines

Via S. Biagio and Via Benedetto Croce
Jewellery and religious art.

Via Portalba and the streets around S. Domenico Maggiore
Bookshops and bookbinders.

Piazza Orefici and the alleyways between Corso Umberto and Via Nuova Marina
Jewellery.

Via Catalana
Decorative copper and wrought iron.

OPENING HOURS

As a rule, the opening hours given in this guidebook refer to Monday to Saturday only, but there are variations depending on the type of business and the time of year. Shops open 10.30am-1.30pm/2pm and 4.30pm-7.30pm/8pm, and are closed on Sundays and Monday mornings in winter, and Saturday afternoons in summer. In the Spaccanapoli area and around Via Tribunali, shops are closed on Saturday afternoons all year. Food shops open earlier in the mornings and close on Sundays and Thursday afternoons. Many shops and businesses close for an annual holiday for two weeks around

FINDING YOUR WAY

After each of the addresses in the Shopping and Nightlife sections, a grid reference indicates where to locate the establishment on the map on pp. 82-83.

15 August, and the city may seem a little empty. During the lead-up to Christmas and in May, the shops in the historic centre and around Spaccanapoli are open on Saturdays and Sundays, and some even stay open late. If you want to buy a Neapolitan crib scene or any figurines, it's as well to know that the craftsmen around San Gregorio, who are much in evidence at Christmas, virtually all disappear at all other times of the year, or open much shorter hours.

HOW TO PAY

As tourism has grown, credit cards are increasingly accepted in shops and restaurants. The familiar adhesive stickers displayed on the door will indicate which credit cards are accepted. Shopkeepers sometimes try to encourage you to pay cash, but if you want to use plastic, insist gently. It's a legal requirement that you should be given a receipt (*scontrino* or *ricevuta fiscale*) for any purchase you make, even if it's only a coffee. If the guardia finanza are conducting spot checks and you're caught without a receipt, you're as liable for a fine as the shopkeeper – all part of the war against tax dodgers and the black economy.

BARGAINING

Prices are generally fixed, and shops will often display a sign saying so. It wouldn't be appropriate to try and haggle in clothes or food shops, but, if you feel like it, try your luck with craftsmen, antique and secondhand dealers, and at the flea markets.

SALES

Sales are are held in most shops. The summer sales are in July and mid-September, and the winter ones from mid-January to mid-March. If prices seem suspiciously low, it may be that the shop-keeper is trying to get rid of old models or poor-quality goods.

CUSTOMS

As Italy is a member of the European Union, citizens of the Union are entitled to take home more

or less whatever they want, free of tax, if Value Added Tax has been paid on the purchase. Duty-free sales between EU countries were abolished in June 1999. Be sure to keep keep a receipt for your bigger purchases. It could be useful when clearing customs, or if you ever have to make an

insurance claim. When buying anything valuable, always make sure that both your receipt and the certificate of authenticity state the price of the item and its provenance. The clampdown on fake goods has been stepped up, so without a receipt and certificate of authenticity you may end up having to leave the 'Gucci' bag you've just bought behind.

DELIVERY

Few shops deliver furniture or works of art overseas. If you require overseas delivery, you'll need to use a specialised transport company. Here are the addresses of reliable companies:

Tir Air Cargo
Via A. Depretis, 145 -
☎ 081 551 20 30
Züst - Ambrosetti
Via A. Vespucci, 78
☎ 081 553 59 19
Danzas
Via S. Salvatore, 2 (à Casoria)
☎ 081 772 01 11.

DEPARTMENT STORES

La Rinascente
Via Toledo, 343
☎ 081 41 15 11
Standa
Via Solimene, 143
☎ 081 578 04 08
Upim
Via Diaz-Piazza Matteotti, 7
☎ 081 552 12 79
Via dei Mille, 59,
☎ 081 41 75 20
Coin
Via Santa Caterina a Chiaia, 23
☎ 081 245 19 38

WOMEN'S FASHION

When it comes to ladies' fashion, Naples may not be Rome or Milan, but it does offer plenty of original ideas and talented designers. So whether you want the boutiques of top Italian designers in Piazza dei Martiri, or the more inexpensive clothes of Via Toledo, here are some addresses for both Neapolitan haute couture and attractive ready-to-wear clothes. There's a great deal to choose from.

DESIGNER BOUTIQUES

Prada

Via Calabritto, 9 (B3)
☎ 081 764 13 23
Mon.-Sat.
10am-2pm, 4-8pm.

This long, narrow boutique is minimalist in style, like the clothes themselves. Prada was founded in 1913 in Milan, and owed its early success to bags made of parachute material. Nowadays you'll find everything from the smallest accessory to evening gowns, all with those distinctive Prada qualities – elegant simplicity of cut and excellent quality of both material and workmanship. The 'Prada woman' is sophisticated without being showy. If you appreciate minimalist chic, and your cheque book has no objections, a dress costs around 1.5 million lire, a bag L700,000 and a pair of shoes L500,000.

Versace

Via Calabritto, 7 (B3)
☎ 081 764 42 10
Mon.-Sat.
10am-2pm, 4-8pm.

The Gianni Versace boutique has everything – men and women's fashion, a range of accessories, articles for the home (lovely cushions) – except, perhaps, smiling sales staff. Alongside elegant ladies' suits and black or lamé evening gowns, you'll also find items in vivid yellow-greens. Versace clothes were made to be seen – at a price! Don't expect to find a dress or lady's suit for less than 3 million lire (prices go as high as 7 million lire). The very attractive high-cut jackets in cotton or viscose are 1 million lire.

Max Mara

Piazza Trieste e Trento, 51 (C2)
☎ 081 40 62 42
Mon.-Sat.
10am-2pm, 4-8pm.

Max Mara

The classic elegance of the Max Mara style is famous throughout the world. Nowadays it also includes the more relaxed range of Sport Max and Max Mara Week-End, as well as a range of accessories (sunglasses, fine leather goods and shoes). The boutique is conveniently located, spacious, airy and smart. Well-informed sales assistants are always at hand to help you with a ready smile –

something you won't find everywhere you go in Naples. Your choice ranges from the cashmere coat – a famous Max Mara item – for 1.5 million lire, to the key-ring for L100,000.

DESIGNERS

Amina Rubinacci

Via dei Mille, 16 (B2)
☎ 081 30 48/081 41 56 72
Mon.-Sat.
10am-1.30pm, 4.30-8pm.

Amina Rubinacci's reputation is well-established. In Paris they call her 'the knitwear queen'. Indeed, her pullover a ostrica (literally, 'oyster-style') with the shawl collar that crosses at the front, made her world-famous. Now you'll find this pullover

SWIMMING COSTUMES

Costumi da bagno, or swimming costumes, are made in the small towns at the foot of Vesuvius and exported to many other parts of the world. You find them prominently displayed in shop windows from May to September. Alongside the more classic designs are some you're unlikely to find elsewhere, such as the designs from Occhi Verdi, and the more sophisticated versions from La Perla. They also come in outlandish gold variations or with artificial flowers for those who want to be noticed. Many have been conceived for sunbathing rather than for swimming. You could try the following addresses:

Donadio (May-Sep.)
Via Duomo, 12 (C1)
☎ 081 44 97 62

Franceschi
Via Chiaia, 216 (B2)
☎ 081 40 69 09

in a variety of classic colours – burgundy, plum, pale blue, white, grey and black (L120,000-150,000). They're displayed alongside beautiful long knitwear coats and a range of woollen jackets (L450,000). Amina's daughter, Federica, has designed a more youthful line of closer fitting, shorter, more décolleté clothes.

Alessio Visone

Via M. d'Alaya, 6 (B2)
☎ 081 42 13 90
By appointment.

Alessio is probably Naples' most famous designer. His themed catwalk shows, staged in the most unusual locations – industrial buildings, railway stations or even in the Castel dell'Ovo – always create a stir. If you're after the dress of your dreams, go up to the 4th floor where, in the plain white decor of his apartment, Alessio himself will design and sketch just such a dress before your very eyes. Then you can watch him cut it out from the natural fibres he loves so much – silk, linen or cashmere. Expect to pay no less than 1.5 million lire for a lady's suit, 2 million lire for an evening gown, and to wait 1-2 weeks for delivery. This charismatic Neapolitan designer's motto is 'Woman, and not only a woman', so expect clothes that are sensual and practical at the same time.

READY-TO-WEAR

Giussani

Via S. Pasquale, 82 (B2)
☎ 081 40 64 81
Mon.-Sat.
10am-1.30pm, 4.30-8pm.

The boutique is decorated in black and white, and has taken the leopard as its symbol. That says it all, as the style here is both sexy and feline. Ida, the designer, also likes to play on the transparency of a particular material, such as the chinks in wide-meshed knitwear, which can then be worn over a body or T-shirt. She also likes to use glitter. Her speciality is the evening dress (L200,000-800,000), but you'll find all kinds of clothes and accessories, from a roadworthy snakeskin helmet to more classic ladies' suits (L500,000-1.2 million).

Melinoi and the Chinese Company

Via B. Croce, 34 (C2)
☎ 081 552 12 04
Mon.-Sat.
10am-1.30pm, 4.30-7.30pm.

Don't be put off by the rather unusual name. There's nothing Chinese about this shop, which sells some of the most interesting clothes available in the historic centre. Neither should you pay too much attention to the display in the window, as there are many reasonably-priced items inside. You'll also find young lines by the new generation of Italian designers (Philosophy, Gigli, Transit, Seventy, One Way and others). There's plenty of choice, ranging from flowing linen dresses for the summer (L250,000) to well-cut outfits for the autumn (L500,000).

Staffelli

Via C. Poerio, 12 (B3)
☎ 081 764 69 22
Mon.-Sat. 10am-1.30pm, 4-8pm.

Staffelli isn't only a boutique, it's also a way of life – life according to Anabella Esposito. The interior is tiled, sober and inviting. Here you'll be welcomed like an old friend, and should immediately feel at home. You'll be invited to try on whatever you like and offered excellent advice without being made to feel you have to buy anything – though you'll probably succumb. All the latest fashions are here, but in a toned-down, more minimalist version. The clothes by Romeo Gigli, Spirit and Sergio Zambon have all been chosen by Ernesto, a clothes designer for over 30 years, and a one-time friend of Andy Warhol.

Pour Les Amis

Via Alabardieri, 23 (B3)
☎ 081 41 33 57
Mon.-Sat.
10am-1.30pm, 4.30-8pm.

The name of the shop ('for our friends') is in itself an invitation and a statement of intent. The Petirro trio set out to extend their clients a friendly welcome and even the prices are friendly. You'll find really attractive jumpers and shirts in original designs with slogans in bright colours and a slightly masculine cut (L80,000-160,000). The range of leather goods might also prove tempting, and picks up on the designs of the cotton and silk ties. Bags start at L120,000.

Maxi-Ho

Via N. Nisco, 20 (B2)
☎ 081 42 75 30
Mon.-Sat. 10am-1.30pm.

Massimiliano Coppola was one of the first in Naples to start selling Italian designer clothes that combined traditional elegance with the latest fashions. So expect to see clothes by Prada and Gucci alongside those of Jil Sander, Donna Karan, Costum National, D.K.N.Y. and the ever-present Dolce & Gabbana. Prices for a lady's suit range from L350,000-2 million lire. The mercatino versions (i.e. unlabelled) are on sale two doors down.

Studio Rog

Via Carducci, 38 (B3)
☎ 081 41 74 27
Mon.-Sat. 10am-1.30pm, 4.30-7.30pm.

Studio Rog began by selling simply-designed leather bags whose appeal relied on the quality of the leather. They made their name with a large soft leather pouch (L300,000-350,000) based on the shape of a folded pocket handkerchief. Nowadays, Giulio and Rosanna Pane also sell excellent-quality

clothes. You'll find simple designs, both classic and casual (by such designers as Cantarelle, Rebecchi, and Scapa), in a range of prices (ladies' suits cost L400,000-1.5 million lire).

Giorgio Abbigliamento

Via Calabritto, 29 (B3)
☎ 081 764 69 22
Mon.-Sat.
10am-1.30pm, 4-7.30pm

This shop sells clothes for women aged 20-50 looking for a smart middle-class look. The Estrenese label is sporty casualwear; Bensussan couture is a line of elegant clothes for women, and Agnona is the cashmere range. In the way of shirts, Giorgio stocks the very popular Asperi range (classic English cut, with mother-of-pearl button cuffs and hand-stitched 'Neapolitan shoulders'). For the past 15 or so years, the name Giorgio abbigliamento has been synonymous with quality (L100,000 for a blouse or a scarf, 1.5 million lire for a cashmere coat). The men's department is upstairs.

DESIGNER SECONDS

Mercato Margherita

Via Verdi 6 (C2)
☎ 081 40 20 24
Mon.-Sat.
10am-1.30pm, 4-8pm.

The Barbaro clothes chain houses its permanent sale in what was once the Margherita salon, hence the furnishings – lacquered oriental furniture, ironwork fittings and unusual old objects. The clothes on sale are by Jean-Paul Gaultier, Lolita Lempicka, Lacroix and Les Copains, as well as Italian labels, such as Moschino and Dolce & Gabbana. The latest designer seconds sell for 70% of their original price. On older collections, reductions can be as much as 70%, though you won't be buying the last word in fashion.

Chi Cerca Trova

Via Fiorelli, 3 (B3)
☎ 081 764 28 09
Mon.-Sat.
9am-1pm, 4.30-8pm.

Giuseppe Violante sells clothes that haven't sold well either this year or last in other shops, as well as classic designs from the last two or three years. You'll find all the top Italian designer labels at reasonable prices (which are also sometimes negotiable). The premises themselves are worth a look, the shop is housed in an old 1920s villa with

VIA TOLEDO OR VIA CHAIA – CHEAP OR CHIC?

The shops in both these streets specialise exclusively in clothes, many of which are made locally. That said, the two streets are very different. Start in Via Toledo (C2) where you'll find reasonably-priced clothes for young people, though the quality can vary, especially in shops that entice clients with misleading sconti (sales). The shops become smarter as you near Piazza Trieste e Trento (C2) and Via Chiaia (B2), and here you'll find attractive and affordable ready-to-wear. The most exclusive shopping area begins just after the bridge.

large Art Deco-style drawing rooms and a garden, as well as a bar to keep clients happy.

CLOTHES SIZES

While you're busy hunting for that incredibly chic little black number, don't forget that clothes sizes in Italy are different from those at home (for both women and men). Most sales assistants will be able to help you find the perfect fit, but we've compiled easy conversion tables on p. 126 to ensure that the outfit of your dreams not only looks amazing but fits well.

FINE LEATHER GOODS

The leather goods you see displayed in shop windows will probably have come from a nearby factory. The range of goods on offer is immense, and includes everything from the classic styles and good quality to be found in Via Duomo or Via Chiaia to designer products exported the world over. A stay in Naples is a good opportunity to find a bag that's well made and doesn't cost a fortune.

Mario Valentino
Via Calabritto, 10 (B3)
☎ 081 764 42 62
Mon.-Sat.
10am-1.30pm, 4-8pm.

The shoes on sale here are so original they wouldn't look out of place in the Museum of Modern Art in New York. Valentino likes to combine traditionally incompatible materials, such as leather and plastic, to make shoes that are exactly what a stylish woman looking for something a little out of the ordinary might want. Prices for a bag or pair of shoes start at L250,000.

Ramirez
Via Calabritto, 18 (B3)
☎ 081 245 20 98
Mon.-Sat.
10am-1.30pm, 4-8pm.

The logo for this shop selling elegant, casual and sports shoes, is an 'R' in the shape of a shoe. Though the shop only opened in 1997, the Ramirez label has existed for over 60 years and is exported all over the world. Classic and modern shoes start at L190,000.

L'Artigiano, Sandali
Vico Belledonne a Chiaia, 23 (B2)
Mon.-Sat. 9am-1.30pm, 4-8pm.

This small workshop and shoemaker's was once a favourite with Jackie Kennedy. The Ricci family has been producing handmade made-to-measure sandals here for the past 50 years. You'll have to wait four

days before you can collect your own pair (L50,000-180,000). One of the most attractive designs is the *caprese*, which is very open, with flat heels, and resembles the sandals worn by the ancient Romans.

Pistola Guanti
Via S. Caterina a Chiaia, 12 A (B2)
☎ 081 42 20 58
Mon.-Sat.
10am-1.30pm, 4.30-8pm.

Pistola has never yet succumbed to passing fashions, and instead continues to offer a wide range of gloves all made in Naples. Apart from the

more traditional designs, there are elbow-length gloves and made-to-measure gloves. Prices start at L30,000.

Aldo Tramontano

Via Chiaia, 149 (B2)
☎ 081 41 48 37
Mon.-Sat.
10am-2pm, 4-8pm.

The business started in 1865 and stayed in the Tramontano family until 1997. However, little has changed since. Its faithful clientele includes Woody Allen, Tom Cruise and Pavarotti, among many others. Here, all the bags, suitcases and

accessories – including the famous Tramontano wallet – are made from natural materials (leather, but also wood, bamboo and seashells). The handworked wolf's head seen on the belts is the emblem of the brand. A wallet or belt costs around L130,000.

Idem-Maktub

Via Chiaia, 194 (B2)
☎ 081 40 74 71
Every day
10am-1.30pm, 4.30-7.30pm.

The Idem label represents novelty born of tradition. That is to say, the younger generation's desire to widen the product range and capitalise on the Tramontano family's century-old reputation for quality leather goods. The label currently sells bags and belts, as well as clothes, jewellery and decorative items. All are made from high-quality materials and are designed in-house. Items are on display in the upstairs workshop, which also has a selection of one-off creations.

Isaia

Via Bisignano, 20 (B3)
☎ 081 764 39 86
and 081 764 23 22
Mon.-Sat. 10am-1.30pm,
4.30-8pm.

This shop is owned by the friendly Anna Isaia, and if you're looking for a soft, comfortable suede shirt, you've come to the right place. Since Anna took over the family business, which has specialised in luxury furs since 1904, she's added a range of artificial furs, as well as leather clothing for men and women. An unlined shirt costs L300,000.

Alta Moda Pirone

Via San Pasquale, 29 (B2)
☎ 081 41 19 27
Mon.-Sat.
9am-1.30pm, 3.30-7.30pm.

The business has been in the family for three generations and is now run by Delia and Mimmo Pirone. Its founder, Antonio Puzzone, started it in 1906. The royal family, whose coats were edged with astrakhan, numbered among his

customers. Today Alta Moda Pirone still sells furs, which it displays alongside cashmere coats and silk raincoats.

MEN'S FASHION

Refined elegance is the characteristic feature of Italian fashion for men, so now's your chance to buy an item of clothing distinguishable by its cut, colours and quality of finishing. In fact, so-called classic styles are becoming ever more inventive, and leisurewear is increasingly acquiring a touch of class, or, as the Italians say, *tocco di classe.*

Eddy Monetti

Via dei Mille, 45 (B2)
☎ **081 40 47 07**
and 081 40 70 64
Mon.-Sat.
9.30am-1.30pm, 4.30-8pm.

There's a place in every smart wardrobe for a classic elegant tailor-made 3-button suit (1.3-2.5 million lire). The Eddy Monetti boutique is especially well-known in Italy for its fabulous cashmere garments and short padded overcoats with cashmere linings, which are currently very popular.

Mariano Rubinacci

Via dei Mille, 1 (B2) and
Via G. Filangieri, 26 (B2)
☎ **081 40 39 08**
Mon.- Sat.
10am-1.30pm, 4.30-8pm.

This tailor and shirt-maker made his name in the 1930s, at a time when his soberly-cut suits and

shirts became popular with the Italian writer Malaparte and film director Vittorio De Sica, among others. The premises are labyrinthine in layout, and also offer a vast range of ready-to-wear clothing. The shop is worth a visit for both its cashmeres and its made-to-order ties (L90,000-120,000).

Gutteridge & Co

Via Toledo,188/193 (C2)
☎ **081 552 15 18**
Mon.-Sat.
10am-1.30pm,
4.30-8pm.

It's in the magnificent Palazzo Stigliano that English tradition and Neapolitan tailoring meet. This was the first establishment to offer top-quality ready-to-wear men's clothes in Naples, and is a good place to buy yourself an Italian-styled suit made from British cloth (from L400,000 upwards).

Blasi

Via dei Mille, 27/35 (B2)
☎ **081 41 52 83**
Mon.-Sat. 10am-1.30pm,
4.15-8pm.

Blasi offers well-cut, tasteful clothes, all made from the finest materials, and with a hint of fashion. Even the ready-to-wear range is hand finished. However, their most famous garment is without a doubt the bespoke suit, which goes so well with a perfectly-fitting Blasi shirt and elegant tie.

Marino

Via S. Caterina a Chiaia,
73/75 (B2)
☎ **081 41 62 34**
Mon.-Sat.
10am-1.30pm, 4.30-8pm.

The founder, Giuseppe Marino, was once milliner to the royal household before turning his hand to clothes. The shop is now run by his grandson and only sells the Marino family label. The clothes are good-quality leisurewear and

reasonably priced (cotton gabardine jackets sell for L280,000).

Luciano Coppola

Via dei Mille 47
ABC (B2)
☎ **081 41 30 26**
Mon.-Sat. 10am-
1.30pm, 4.30-
8pm.

If you're not sure what to buy, ask one of the capable sales assistants. The clothes on sale range from the fairly classic to the more relaxed, and labels include Brando, Iceberg, Fusco and Gigli. Expect to spend L140,000-360,000 for a pair of trousers, and L800,000-3 million lire for a suit. There's also an attractive selection of leather clothes that are truly waterproof thanks to a special treatment.

Emporio Armani

Piazza Trieste e Trento,
50 (C2)
☎ **081 41 80 37**
Mon.-Sat.
10am-1.30pm, 4.30-8pm.

If you're looking for an elegant Italian look, at a price, of course, you can dress yourself literally from head to toe (not forgetting accessories) in Armani. This comfortable modern range of clothes aimed at the 15-35 age group includes a wide variety of shoes, vests, shirts (L90,000) and trousers and has proved a big success.

Anna Matuozzo

Viale Gramsci,
26 I (A3)
☎ **081 66 38 74**
Mon.-Sat.
9am-6pm.

All the shirts at Anna Matuozzo's are handmade and guaranteed for life. The stiff collar and itchy cuffs that so often come with industrially-manufactured shirts have become a thing of

the past here. If the Rolls-Royce in shirts is the only thing for you, just take along your measurements (a single fitting will suffice), a handful of banknotes and leave your forwarding address.

PANICO

Via Carducci, 29 (B2)
☎ **081 41 58 04**
Mon.-Sat.
10am-1.30pm, 4.30-8pm.

There's no point in thinking that you know what's best for you as Signor Panico knows better. No matter what your shape, the clothes can be cut to fit you like a glove. The cut is ageless, and suits he made 15 years ago still look as if they were made yesterday – which is just as well since they cost an awe-inspiring 1.8-3 million lire. You'll need two fittings before the suit of your dreams can be sent to you.

MEN'S ACCESSORIES

An attractive tie, a good pair of shoes and, on occasion, a hat, are the making of a man, as well as subtle clues to his personality. The Italians, who take particular care of their appearance, know this better than most. Naples offers the best in traditional ties and hats, as well as smaller and more unusual and accessories to add that perfect finishing touch.

Marinella
Via Riviera di Chiaia, 287 (B3)
☎ 081 764 42 14
Mon.-Sat.
8am-1.30pm. 4-8pm.

If at heart you feel you're a politician, or you're just simply mad about ties, remember there's always a Marinella tie for you. JFK and some of Europe's leading statesmen have all had ties made for them in this small, world-renowned boutique. You can ask Maurizio (carrying on the excellent tradition of his grandfather, Eugenio) to create the perfect tie for you (materials include twill and silk). Prices range from L120,000-150,000 for made-to-order ties, which require three days to make up.

Ricciardi Pipa Club
Piazza Carità, 5 (C2)
☎ 081 552 05 95
Mon.-Sat.
10am-1.30pm, 4-7.30pm.

Owning a meerschaum pipe is quite something. The mineral it's made of gives it a wonderful lightness. The place is a must for dedicated pipe smokers or collectors (and with prices ranging from L18,000-3 million lire, some pipes could arguably be considered works of art). It also has a workshop where they'll repair broken pipes.

E & G Cappelli
Via Cavallerizia a Chiaia, 37 (B2)
☎ 081 552 15 18
Mon.-Sat. 10am-1.30pm, 4.30-7.45pm.

Patrizio works on the old adage that even if a tie is made of precious silk, only care in the making can guarantee its quality. He follows this adage to the letter, as you'll see from the handmade ties on display in his workshop housed in a pretty inner courtyard.

Casa del Cappello

**Corso Umberto I,
202/204 (C2)
☎ 081 28 29 84
Mon.-Sat. 10am-1.30pm,
4-7.30pm.**

Here at
Casa del Cappello,
the heir to a long-established
family business, Signor
Esposito, is carrying on a
tradition of hat-selling.
Among the hundreds of hats
on offer are the
famous *Borsalino*
and *Panizza*.

Il Cappellaio

**Via San Pasquale, 17
(B2)
Mon.-Sat.
10am-1.30pm,
4-7.30pm.**

This could have been the place
for the bowler-hatted city gents
of London not so long ago.
Whether your hat's flattened or
simply dented, Signor Veraldi can
restore it to its original condition.
With a clean and a change of
ribbon, this will cost L40,000.

A real Borsalino costs L300,000,
but for those who find it
cumbersome when not being
worn, there's now also a unisex
roller version, which can simply
be rolled up to fit inside a bag.

Peluso

**Via Alabardieri, 29 (B3)
☎ 081 42 14 06
Mon.-Sat.
10am-1.30pm, 4-8pm.**

Peluso, the home of the
gentleman's shoe, has
been making
handmade
shoes

for loyal clients who insist on the
best since 1907. The premises are
low-lit and inviting, and also
cater for women who want
perfect-fitting shoes (L300,000-
400,000).

Vic Matié

**Via V. Colonna, 37/38 (B2)
☎ 081 40 57 12
Mon.-Sat.
9.45am-1.30pm, 4-8pm.**

Though founded only recently,
the Vic Matié label has already
established a reputation in
Paris and Milan. The men's
range is designed by Paul May
and the women's by Vic Matié.
The style is trendy but sober for
a young clientele with resolutely
modern tastes (L180,000-
350,000).

FOOTBALL HEAVEN

If by any chance you're
a diehard fan of the
Italian team Juventus ('Juvé'
to fans) or AC Milan, or
you've promised a present
to your nephew who's mad
about Ronaldo, Piazza
Garibaldi (D1) is the place
to come. There are all kinds
of roadside stalls (some more
legal than others) selling
the shirts of many famous
Italian and foreign players
for as little as L25,000
(L20,000, if you know how
to haggle).

FOR BABIES AND CHILDREN

No-one can blame the Neapolitans for the sharp decline in the Italian birth rate. In Naples you'll see children (some better behaved than others) running about everywhere, along side streets and in and out of the trees in the Villa Comunale park. As you might expect, there are also plenty of shops catering for their every need.

Peter Pan
Via Filangieri, 25 (B2)
☎ **081 42 12 71/**
081 40 54 58
Mon.-Sat.
10am-2pm, 4-8pm.

Peter Pan has been setting the standard in children's clothes for the past 50 years in Naples. The emphasis is on fashionable clothes for children, but with traditional styles too. English-style coats, tartan kilts and embroidered garments (starting at L220,000) for a classic look, as well as the latest Armani and Scapa designs for connoisseurs of 0-16 fashion.

La Bancarellina
Via Carducci, 39/41 (B3)
☎ **081 40 16 95**
Mon.-Sat.
9.30am-1.30pm,
4.30-8pm.

It's all very well being elegant when you're very young – as long as you're still allowed to run about. That could be the thinking behind La Bancarellina, which sells stylish shoes for the 0-6 age group. Their selection of tough shoes includes the Mini Man, Le Guignol and Start-Rite labels. There are also some lovely hand-embroidered designs by Nicoletta Faina using traditional methods that should satisfy even the most fashion-conscious toddler.

Siola
Via Chiaia, 111/115 (B2)
☎ **081 41 50 36**
Mon.-Sat. 10am-
1.30pm, 4.30-8pm.

Siola opened in 1937, is laid out in different sections to suit different tastes A soft-hued corner sells the Milan-based Sophie Petit (0-8 age group) range, while a vividly-painted corner houses the bright colours of Miki House. Prices range from L19,000 for a T-shirt to 3 million lire for a christening robe.

Sciuscià

Via Vittoria Colonna, 3 (B2)
☎ 081 40 39 38, Mon.-Sat. 10am-1.30pm, 4-8pm.

Sciuscià has a range of clothes guaranteed to win over even the most difficult children, i.e. those who already feel a little grown up. All the clothes on display are the latest designs –

Etro and Ralph Lauren polo shirts (L78,000), Gant jackets (from L160,000) and outfits by Simonetta. In short, excellent-quality clothes for those who want to look their best at the nursery.

La Girandola

Via Roma, 400 (C2)
☎ 081 552 15 53
Mon.-Sat. 10am-1.45pm, 4-8pm.

This shop sells not only a whole range of toys, but also furniture and other articles for children's rooms, all handmade in a local Neapolitan workshop. The Lilliputian furniture is made of wood and comes in bright colours, with motifs such as stars and cartoon characters.

Pepot

Via G. Merliani, 86 (A2)
☎ 081 578 03 24
Mon.-Sat. 10am-1.15pm, 4.30-8pm.

This tiny shop is filled with beautiful furry animals and rag dolls, which are the house speciality. They're handmade, and come in all sizes and colours. You can even watch them being made and order them to your specifications (they take 2-7 days). Prices range from L10,000 to L95,000 for the larger models (1.10m/3ft high).

CLEVER ADDRESSES

Naples is far from being well organised regarding activities for children. Nor are parents helped by the traffic, pollution and lack of open and green spaces. So, in case you don't find any of your own, here are a few ideas.

For children and adults:
Parks: Capodimonte park (see p.50), Villa Floridiana (see p. 46), Villa Comunale (see p. 45).
Amusement Parks: Edenlandia, Viale Kennedy (ferrovia Cumana, Edenlandia exit), ☎ 081 239 40 90).
Kennedy Minigolf: Via Camillo Guerra, 60 (☎ 081 587 13 86).

For children only:
The Iterate Association Looks after children who hate shopping and museums (☎ 081 552 65 03, 9.30am-7.30pm).
Mini Club Amedeo (Piazza Amedeo I, ☎ 081 41 18 85).

La Città del Sole

Via Kerbaker, 46 (B2)
☎ 081 578 14 80
Mon.-Sat. 10am-1.30pm, 4.30-8pm.

As soon as you come into this shop you know you've entered a world without Barbie dolls or toy guns. All the toys here are made of wood, and have a timeless appeal. Not only are they decorative, they're also educational and displayed according to the skills they develop – building, discovery and dexterity. For older children, there are the highly original puzzles.

FOR TEENAGERS

Given that unemployment of under-25s is as high as 60%, this might not be the sector of society with the most disposable income. Yet no-one wants to look like their parents, and everyone still wants to look good for the opposite sex and to impress their friends – so life's not that simple. Here are a few of the many places in Naples where you can attend to your image.

Magazzini Generali
Via dei Mille, 26/28 (B2)
☎ 081 41 83 72
Mon.-Sat.
10am-1.30pm, 4-8pm.

Magazzini is well known as a place to go to buy good leisurewear without spending too much. Here you'll find Warner Brothers T-shirts (L35,000), blouson-style jackets, tight-fitting and bell-bottom trousers and shoes with soles thick enough to irritate your parents. There's also a wide range of gadgets, such as fluorescent stars for your bedroom ceiling (L12,000).

Pizzeria Jeanseria
Via Roma, 367 (C2)
☎ 081 551 46 43
Mon.-Sat.
9.30am-8.15pm.

Pizzeria Jeanseria sometimes runs a special offer of a free pizza for every item bought. They sell a huge array of Charro, Lee and Levi clothing and accessories. A pair of Levi 501s costs L110,000, and shirts L95,000, possibly with a meal thrown in!

Pourquoi Pas ?
Via S. Pasquale a Chiaia, 68 (B2)
☎ 081 41 31 60
Mon.-Sat.
10am-1.30pm, 4-8pm.

If your ego needs a little boost, why not have your face on a T-shirt (L35,000), hat, mug or even jigsaw (L35,000)? All you have to do is take the picture of your choice along and Pourquoi Pas (literally, 'Why Not') will do the rest. You could also have your very own souvenir video made up – by having your holiday photos edited onto a video complete with Neapolitan background music. If you're short of ideas, this is the place to come.

Original Marine's

Via dei Mille, 83 A (B2) or Via Roma, 208-209 (C2)
☎ 081 41 39 68/40 09 69
Mon.-Sat. 10am-1.30pm, 4-8pm.

The trick is to tell the other members of your party there's something for everyone in this family store. It's true – they stock clothes for everyone, from items for the new-born to sporty casualwear for adults. The various sections are arranged according to age-group, but what they all have in common is Original Marine's speciality, the sweatshirt. Everything is good quality and attractively-priced (from L29,000), so everyone should be happy.

Bamba

Via Chiaia, 209 (B2)
☎ 081 41 47 67
Mon.-Sat. 10am-2pm, 4.30-8pm.

Walk past the shop windows with their intriguing displays into an inner courtyard, where you'll find Bamba. What distinguishes these clothes is the original use of materials and colours – green imitation reptile skin, delicate silver threads and enough little details to set you apart from the crowd. Long and short dresses from L120,000, trousers from L100,000 and costume jewellery from L30,000. The secondhand clothes shop and discount store at Via Chiatamone, 21-22 is also worth a look.

Invicta

Via Chiaia 147 (B2)
☎ 081 41 62 60
Mon.-Sat. 10am-1.30pm, 4.30-8pm.

The Italians call a rucksack a *zainetto*, and the ones made by Invicta are everywhere. These distinctive brightly-coloured rucksacks are almost indestructible, even if crammed with books, and, despite their popularity, they've remained reasonably priced (from L70,000). Just the thing to cut a dash on the way to school and between classes.

MÙ MÙ FREQUENCIES

Piazza Monteoliveto, 10 (C2)
☎ 081 552 41 03
Tue.-Sun. 11am-2pm, 4-8pm, bar 11pm-4am.

It all happens in the basement at Mù Mù, in a decor of metal-clad walls and exposed piping. By day, the action's in the shop, but by night it's in the bar. The clothes on sale here are all old clothes that have been recycled, re-coloured, re-cut and reassembled to create something entirely new. The rucksacks (L20,000-50,000) are particularly unusual, with seatbelts for straps. If only everyone had this much imagination! Mù Mù also sells kites, video games, CDs and records. This is where Neapolitan DJs come to stock up on house, trans, techno and the latest sounds in general. From 11pm onwards you can come and listen to music and have a drink. Hip hop is on Tuesdays, techno on Thursdays and softer sounds on Sundays. You'll need a membership card, but it only costs L10,000 and is valid for a year.

INTERIOR DECORATION: DESIGN MEETS TRADITION

Neapolitan homes tend to be decorated fairly traditionally, often with a wide variety of furniture styles and objects. Nevertheless, you'll find furniture shops stocking those clean modern designs that have launched the reputations of a number of contemporary Italian designers. And while such minimalist designs occasionally seem a little austere, they can be matched with more colourful utilitarian objects and warmer-toned textiles.

Novelli Arredamento

Piazza Amedeo, 21/22 (B2)
☎ **081 41 32 33**
and 081 41 53 50
Mon.-Sat.
10am-2pm, 4-8pm.

When designers are as talented and inventive as those behind the Kartell label, even the most commonplace objects start to seem extraordinary. Good examples include the famous Book

Worm or Lovely Rita flexible book shelves by Ron Arad (L350,000) and the magazine-holders by Giotto Stoppino or Philippe Starck.

Holt

Via Filangieri, 56 (B2)
☎ **081 41 80 67**
Mon.-Sat.
10am-1.30pm, 4.30-8pm.

If you don't feel you could ever part with your old Chesterfield sofa, pay a visit instead to the lighting department in the basement, or have a look at the soft furnishings

(some in very summery patterns) and *porcellana bianca*. Holt is chock-full of ingenious practical items, such as a honey-pourer that can also be used for chocolate, a sauceboat with two lips for thick and thin sauces (L27,000) and a *mozzarella* dish.

Croff

Via A. Diaz, 32 (C2)
☎ **081 552 39 83**
Mon.-Sat.
9.30am-1.30pm, 4-7.30pm.

Croff is a treasure trove of household objects made in Italy.

Among these treasures are Vietri ceramic tea cups (L12,000), lamps made exclusively for Croff by a local craftsman and reproductions of Old Masters on canvas. This is the kind of shop it's difficult to leave empty-handed. An international delivery service is available.

Il Pellicano

Via Duomo, 217 (C1)
☎ 081 20 48 89
Mon.-Sat.
10am-1.30pm,
4-8pm.

This shop contains a higgledy-piggledy assortment of fine articles for the home and is a great source of presents. Amid all the wickerwork, wrought iron, wood and crockery, you'll also find, at very modest prices (from as little as L1000), trays and lights for outside the house.

Bassetti

Piazza Trieste e Trento, 44 (C2)
☎ 081 41 17 42
Via Scarlatti, 209 D
☎ 556 15 86
Mon.-Sat.
10am-1.30pm, 4.30-8pm.

Bassetti is Italy's leading name in household linen. They have styles to suit all tastes, from the most classic to the latest design. The 'photo sheets' appear to be all the rage at the moment – so if you want to wake up in the middle of the Arctic amid ice fields of romping polar bears, Bassetti have just the sheets for you.

Au Passamentier

Via G. Carducci, 27 (B3)
☎ 081 551 33 63
Mon.-Sat.
10am-1.30pm, 4.30-8pm.

Since 1963, Au Passamentier has been the place to buy braid, cords and fringes of every kind (L20,000-50,000/m/yd). It also has a wide choice of traditional furnishing fabrics, all high-quality and made by famous Italian names, such as Lisio, Fadini and Borghi (L30,000-300,000/myd).

DOING SOME DECORATING?

Naples has no shortage of shops selling fine furnishing fabrics. You'll find an excellent choice of brocades, damasks, Jacquard weaves and English prints, all at a wide range of prices. Almost all the fabrics are 140cm/54in wide, and you'll need about 5m/yd of material for an armchair, and approximately twice the height of the window for a set of curtains. Aside from the addresses already given, Marra has a fine selection of ready-made curtains, all hemstitched by hand (Via G. Carducci, 2, B3 ☎ 764 57 39, Mon.-Sat. 10am-1.30pm, 4.30-8pm).

Marcello D'Amato

Via Donnalbina, 37 (C2)
☎ 081 25 14 091
Mon.-Sat.
9am-1.30pm,
2.30-7pm.

Marcello has a magic touch when it comes to coloured glass. Using traditional techniques, he makes all sorts of one-off glass objects with lead (for the glass panels), bronze or aluminium joints. His speciality is lamps (from L100,000), for which there are also matching candleholders, mirrors and boxes (from L30,000).

DECORATIVE CERAMICS

The production of decorated ceramic crockery, vases, jars and tiles is a craft that dates back to the 14th century. The most renowned examples still come from Vietri, a small village on the Amalfi coast, which is probably the best place to buy them. However, as you'll see on your travels about Naples, there are many ceramics workshops (some also schools) in the city itself, each displaying its own style.

Bottega di ceramiche qualche arredo e altre piccole cose
Via C. Poerio, 40 (B2)
☎ 081 764 26 26
Mon.-Sat.
10am-1.30pm, 4.30-8pm.

The decorated ceramic tradition in Caltagirone, a small village in Sicily, dates back to the ancient Greeks. Even nowadays, the work is still carried out entirely by hand, using traditional techniques that are a well-guarded secret. The fish-shaped bottle is designed to be used without glasses (L50,000). You'll find many other examples of this *arte povera* here.

La Soffitta
Via B. Croce, 12 (C2)
☎ 081 551 63 39
Mon. and Wed. 10am-12.30pm,
Tue. and Thu. 4-7pm.

Anna Maria Pondrano Altavilla's school of decorative ceramic art is, as its name ('the attic') suggests, housed right under the eaves, of the Palazzo Croce – one of the most beautiful settings in the historic centre. Anna Maria herself will be delighted to show you how a ceramic object 'is born', and also show you some of her own work.

Lisa Weber
Via G. Paladino, 4 (C2)
Mon.-Sat.
10am-1.30pm, 5-8pm.

In her workshop and showroom, Lisa Weber still uses a pedal-driven potter's wheel, a method that

belongs to bygone days. For the past 20 years, she's been making attractive stoneware and terracotta kitchen utensils. She also makes purely decorative objects using browns, greys and dark blues – hardly the traditional Mediterranean colours.

Il Cantuccio della Ceramica

Via B. Croce, 38 (inside courtyard-C2)
☎ **081 552 58 57**
Mon.-Fri. 10am-6pm, Sat. morn.

The Cantuccio della Ceramica is both a showroom and a cultural organisation (of which there are many in Naples) whose stated aim is to promote and teach the delicate art of ceramic pottery. Among the many attractive items on sale are lampshades, ashtrays and pots, all decorated with beautiful friezes and geometric patterns.

La Bottega dell'Arte

Via Catena 2/4, in Capri
☎ **081 837 18 78**
Mon.-Sat.
8am-1pm, 4-8pm.

Some of this workshop's larger vases are now on permanent

exhibition in the Met in New York, and examples of its ceramic tables and benches can be seen in Piazza A. Diaz. The workshop also has a pleasant garden and fountain decorated with sculptures you can admire at your leisure. All the items are unique creations, and include clocks (L200,000-400,000) and small

plates (from L20,000), many of which are scaled-down versions of larger designs.

Ceramiche Artistiche Solimene

Via Madonna degli Angeli, 7, à Vietri
☎ **089 21 02 43**
Mon.-Fri. 8am-6pm
Sat. morn.

This is one of the best-known ceramics workshops in Vietri, and hence always full of tourists. The choice of items on offer is immense, and includes beautiful oval plates ideal for pasta (from L5,000).

Russo e Figli

Via Bisignano, 51 (B3)
☎ **081 764 83 87**
Mon.-Sat. 9am-6pm.

Don Mimi and his sons work with stone, and perpetuate an age-old tradition. These true craftsmen

draw on Ancient Greece and Rome, as well as the Renaissance, for their designs, many of which take the form of friezes, masks or tables and can be made in Brazilian blue granite, Pakistani onyx or marble from Verona. The rear of the showroom is nothing short of a treasure trove.

VIETRI, THE CERAMICS MUSEUM

Torretta di Villa Guariglia, Vietri
☎ **089 21 18 35**
Every day
9am-1pm, 3-7pm.

The majolica-decorated dome and bell tower of the church of San Giovanni Battista echo the contents of the museum. Vietri was once called the *maiolicari* district. Its workshops were famous for producing ceramics with religious motifs, many beautiful specimens of which are still to be found in the streets, churches and *palazzi* of the region, as well as inside the museum itself. Vietri remains the best place to buy ceramics – as the shop windows prove.

ORIGINAL ITEMS

The following section includes all the shops where it's a pleasure simply to wander in and browse. You'll find many small typically Neapolitan items that make ideal gifts, and are bound to be tempted to treat yourself at the same time.

Napolimania

Via Toledo, 309-312, Borgo Marinara (C2)
☎ 081 41 41 20
Mon.-Sat.
10am-2pm, 4-8pm.

Anyone addicted to Naples can take several precautionary measures before leaving. These include buying a sealed box of Neapolitan

air, or buying the Neapolitan abroad survival kit containing 250gr/9oz of coffee, some genuine Neapolitan water (the only guarantee of a good coffee) and a real Neapolitan *machinetta* with which to combine the two. To further combat nostalgia, watches and T-shirts inscribed with sayings in Neapolitan dialect are also available.

Arethusa

Riviera di Chiaia, 202 C (B3)
☎ 081 41 15 51
Mon.-Sat.
10am-1.30pm, 4.30-8pm.

Those of you who like reproductions of old drawings

and gouaches depicting Naples should pay a visit to Arethusa. Also on sale are limited-edition posters and water-colours by Neapolitan artists (Mario Vitolo and Alessandro Cocchia) for L25,000, as well as much cheaper postcards that don't only show views of the Bay of Naples.

P & C

Largo Vasto a Chiaia, 86 (B2)
☎ 081 41 87 24
Mon.-Sat.
10am-2pm, 4-8pm.

Pasquale Russo's passion is all things miniature. He also collects pens and old share certificates. Items range from the world's smallest pen (3cm), which can be clipped to a buttonhole, to the world's smallest book, whose 10 pages have to be read with a magnifying glass. Other enticing objects include the piccino, a

small notebook with a leather cover to hold business cards and the like, which has proved very popular since it came out in 1990.

Casa della Penna

Corso Umberto 1er, 88 (C2)
☎ 081 20 47 63
Mon.-Sat. 9am-7.30pm.

This shop has been selling pens for three generations. They range from standard pens to the latest designs from well-known brands, but include some collectors' items (for which people pay up to 30 million lire!). So now's your chance to buy a fine example of Italian flair and design, such as the famous Aurora 88, the jewel in the crown of one of

the country's leading companies in the sector (from L420,000).

Lo Scrigno

Via B. Croce, 27-40 (C2)
☎ 081 552 04 64
Mon.-Sat.
10am-1.30pm, 4-7.30pm.

If you've already acquired the Neapolitan habit of wearing an amulet to protect you from the 'evil eye', then you may also want a gold *corno* (horn). These are small and discreet enough to be worn on a chain or bracelet, and Lo Scrigno offers a good selection at low prices (18 carats).

Drogheria Santa Chiara

Via B. Croce, 50 (C2)
☎ 081 551 64 44
Mon.-Sat. 10am-2pm,
4-8pm, open Sun. morn.

People come to this grocery for many reasons. Neapolitans usually come for products brought in from elsewhere. Visitors to Naples are more likely to come for products made in Naples – sauces, jams, Christmas cake, chocolates and limoncello, as well as Vietri pottery (L5,000-60,000), in particular a set of limoncello glasses.

Égraphè

Piazza Miraglia, 391 (C1)
☎ 081 44 62 66
Mon.-Sat.
8.30am-2pm, 5-8pm.

If you're fed up with writing with ordinary biros and felt tips, Égraphè offers you the forgotten pleasures of penholders, handmade paper, personalised seals and watermarked carta d'Amalfi (L21,000-35,000), as well as homemade, perfumed, fluorescent or even 3D inks (from L8,000). Bibliophiles will also find a wide selection of book plates.

Tattoo

Piazzetta Nilo, 15 (C2)
☎ 081 552 09 73
Mon.-Sat. 9am-8pm,
Sun. 10am-2pm.

Tattoo is run by Enzo, Biagio and Massimo, who are all experts in jazz, rock and Neapolitan music. They'll all be happy to point you to something other than O Sole Mio. The music on offer ranges from wonderful 12th-15th century pieces recorded by the Nuova Compagnia di Canto Popolare to more recent music by Murolo, Alma Megretta, 24 Grane and Daniele Sepa. A novel way to learn more about Naples.

Yien

Via Alabardieri, 40 (B3)
☎ 081 41 27 70
Mon.-Sat.
10am-2pm, 4.30-8pm.

The very popular Yien bags are intended for both travelling and everyday use. They're made of leather and micro-fibre and are washable and very strong. However much you mistreat them, they should go on and on (prices start at L130,000).

NEAPOLITAN CRAFTS

Naples owes much of its local colour to its rich variety of craftsmen. Though still working with traditional methods in terracotta, wood or paper, the best craftsmen also invent their own original methods and continue to add to a truly exceptional heritage. There's a variety of crafts on offer, and the workmanship is excellent.

Giuseppe Ferrigno
Via S. Gregorio Armeno, 8 (C1)
☎ 081 552 31 48
Every day 9am-8pm.

The ornamental nativity figurines, angels and Pulcinellas of Giuseppe and Mario have been displayed in New York, Paris and Arles. Their exquisite work draws on 18th-century tradition, combined with their own gifted touch and imagination. The figurines, made of terracotta, wood, polish and silk, (L15,000-600,000) are then used to create scenes from the Naples of the past, though modern celebrities can also feature. The definition of the Christmas crib scene is no longer as strict as it once was.

Di Virgilio
Via S. Gregorio Armeno, 18/20 (C1)
☎ 081 549 16 42
Mon.-Sat. 9am-8pm.

The innumerable ornamental figurines (1-40cm/1/2-16in high) on display either come from the family's century-old workshop or are made by other talented local craftsmen. The 4cm/1½in-high *pastori*

(shepherds) are remarkably well-made and the most expressive of the figurines – though smaller doesn't necessarily mean cheaper (L15,000). They can be bought with *miniature*, tiny items such as baskets filled with food, the best of which are made of wax (L3,000-60,000).

Crèches Gramendola
Via S. Gregorio Armeno, 51 (C1)
☎ 081 551 48 99
Mon.-Sat. 9am-7pm.

Master craftsman Matteo Prencipe's Christmas nativity cribs draw on traditional 19th-century models. Not surprisingly, his workshop is often packed. Cribs

range from the simplest to those with cascades and windmills powered by electricity. The latest design is the fold-up crib that comes complete with all its figurines (L350,000).

Liuteria Calace
Vico S. Domenico Maggiore (C1)
☎ 081 29 36 27
Mon.-Fri.
9am-1pm, 2-4pm.

The Calace family is almost synonymous with the mandolin (L800,000-4 million, 2-3 month wait for an order to be made). For almost two centuries, this family of stringed instrument-makers and musicians has helped to develop the mandolin, both by improving its musical specifications and by composing for the instrument. The shop has other strings to its bow, as it also caters for violinists and guitarists.

Gli artigiani del libro
Calata Trinità Maggiore, 4 (C2)
☎ 081 551 12 80
Mon.-Sat.
8.30am-7pm.

The famous Italian writer Benedetto Croce had his books bound here by Master Eliseo, whose disciples now run the establishment. Such wares as luxury handmade paper and gilded leather bindings prove the high standards of the past have not been lost (from L100,000). Other items that would make attractive gifts include photograph albums and frames, and diaries (L35,000).

Gambardella
Via B. Croce, 28 (C2)
☎ 081 552 08 74
Mon.-Sat. 9am-7pm.

Gambardella sells all kinds of paper for all uses, with 480 types of wrapping paper, boxes and albums in stock. It's a colourful, rustling spectacle laid out on the sagging shelves of an old shop that's been in business for 80 years. You're sure to find the perfect paper here.

Ulisse
Via S. Chiara, 10 A (C2)
☎ 081 552 06 02
Mon.-Sat.
10am-1pm, 4-7pm.

Salvatore Oliva is able to shape and create an expressive face

from a piece of leather. According to him, for this minor miracle to take place, you need more than mere technique – you also need to believe in the restorative power of man's contact with nature, an ancient and increasingly forgotten tradition.

THE NEAPOLITAN CRIB

If you want to arrange your crib in true Neapolitan style, here are some hints. Always bear in mind the principles of perspective – the figurines placed around the central nativity scene should be larger than those on the hillside. Figurines should represent the local populace, from the humble to the prominent – Benino, Ciccibacco, musicians (*zampogna* and *ciaramella*), water-carriers and melon-sellers. The central nativity scene is also an excuse to portray a whole community happy and rejoicing, thus the culinary 'gifts of the lord' (*ben d'iddio*) must also feature, though on many occasions these would have been absent from daily life.

CHEESE AND CHOCOLATE, PASTRIES AND PASTA

You often get the impression that Neapolitans are always eating – any time, anywhere – as if they expected rationing at any moment. The high point of the week is Sunday lunch with the family, a time to see everyone but also to eat. Here are some of the local specialities and the customs that go with them.

Arfé
Via S. Pasquale, 31 (B2)
☎ 081 41 18 22
Mon.-Sat.
8am-1.45pm, 4.30-8pm.

Arfé is the most exclusive food store in Naples. At the cheese counter, you'll find *provola*, soft white cheeses from around Sorrento, *pecorini* (goat's cheese) from Matese, and, of course *mozzarella*. All are delicious. There's also a very tempting range of cooked dishes, such as smoked fish (eel and sturgeon). Little point in trying to resist.

picking out the best mozzarellas for his clients, but also offers delicious alternatives such as *cacciotta al tartuffo* (L28,000/kg/2.2lb), a soft white cheese flavoured with truffles, best appreciated with a slice of white bread and a glass of Piedirosso red wine.

La Montanina
Via Carlo Poerio, 30 (B3)
☎ 081 764 41 81
Mon.-Sat. 8.30am-1.30pm, 4.30-8pm.

The Fusco family have been making cheese for four generations. The family comes from Agerola, a small village near Naples famous for the quality of

Mandara Latticini
Via S. Caterina a Chiaia, 4 (B2)
☎ 081 41 73 78
Mon.-Sat. 8.30am-2.30pm, 4.30-8.30pm.

Mandara's *bufflonne* cheeses (made with buffalo milk) are known throughout the city as cheeses you can rely on. For 30 years, Alessandro Sommella has been

its milk. It's there that they make cheese (delivered each morning before the shop opens) using traditional methods. *Provolone del nonno* ('grandfather's *provolone*') is particularly tasty – it's spicy and full of flavour, and travels well.

Tarallificio Leopoldo

Via Foria, 212 (C1)
☎ **081 45 11 66**
Mon.-Sat. 8.15am-9pm, Sun.
8.15am-2pm, 4-9pm.

Though you may not hear the vendor's call of *taralle, taralle, càvere*, as you once did, these crunchy, salt and peppered biscuits still exist. The recipe of the famous *taralli* biscuit is a closely-guarded secret passed down from generation to generation. You'll also find other delicious traditional Neapolitan biscuits here.

Casa del Tortellino

Via F. Galiani, 30
(inside, mercado della Torretta-not on map)
☎ **081 66 36 06**
Tue.-Sun. 8.30am-8pm, Thu. and Sun. morn. only.

Have you ever wanted to try real Neapolitan pasta at home? If so,

why not buy *ravioli capresi* (the best of all), or *trofie*, *fusilli* or any other kind of homemade pasta (L17,000-25,000/kg/2/2lb), and ask to have them wrapped for travelling. And to avoid any mistakes, make sure you know both the cooking time and the *sugo* ('sauce') recommended for each particular type of pasta. Delicious sauces are also available (L5,000-10,000/500gm/1.1lb).

Gallucci

Via Cisterna dell'Olio 6 C (C2)
☎ **081 551 31 48**
Mon.-Sat. 8am-8pm.

Every Christmas and Easter, this patisserie turns into a chocolate heaven. If there's no room left in your suitcase for chocolate bells and eggs, some of which can be a metre/yard high, then sample a slice of *foresta* – a delicious chocolate log (in mini or maxi sizes, L40,000/kg//2.2lb).

Gay Odin

Via Toledo, 427 (C2)
☎ **081 551 34 91**
Via V. Colonna, 15 B (B2)
☎ **081 41 82 82**
Mon.-Sat.
9.30am-1.30pm, 4.30-8pm.

Once upon a time there was a confectioner named Isidore Odin, who married his assistant Onorina Gay. They lived happily ever after, and founded one of the oldest chocolate-making establishments in Naples. The fairytale continues, as you'll soon see from the display in the Art Nouveau shop window.

WINE, COFFEE AND LIQUEURS

Neapolitans usually drink their coffee standing at the bar. It's a ritual that often takes place two or three times a day, and the café counter is the only place some Neapolitans have breakfast. On the other hand, they're quite prepared to take time over the other meals of the day, often accompanied by local wines, some of which rank alongside the best Italian wines.

Enoteca Belledonne

Vico delle Belledonne
a Chiaia, 18 (B2)
☎ 081 40 31 62
Mon.-Sat. 9am-2pm, 4.30-8pm,
cl. for a fortnight in Aug.

At one time only oil and wine were sold here, but when Antonio and Ciro inherited the business, they decided to turn it into a wine bar. They kept the original decor, and used their skill and experience to make it a bar for those who know their wine. Three times a week, (Thu.-Sat. after 9pm) you can come and taste wines standing at the bar, as customers stood at the counter in the old days.

Caffé Mexico

Piazza Dante, 86 (C1)
☎ 081 549 93 30
Mon.-Sat. 7.30am-8.30pm,
cl. for a fortnight in Aug.

The secret of this bar's success is that the coffee is roasted on the premises. You'll find a wide range of *miscele* (blends), from the most common to the most sophisticated, such as the *vesuvio* (L35,000/kg/2.2lb). Blends also come in attractive, original boxes ideal for packing in suitcases. They make very good presents.

Enoteca Santa Brigida

Via S. Brigida, 77 (C2)
☎ 081 551 39 14
Mon.-Sat.
10am-1.30pm, 4-7.30pm,
cl. for a fortnight in Aug.

Though this *enoteca* (wine bar) has been open for less than five years, Signor Ursini's experience includes a period when he ran one of Naples'

most famous restaurants. As befits a specialist, he'll offer you sound advice, especially on the Italian wines included in the 700 wines kept in stock. Italian wines fall into three categories. The most renowned is

WINES FROM CAMPANIA

WHITE WINES

Lachryma Christi is recognisable by its pale yellow colour, delicate aroma and dry full-bodied flavour that leaves a slightly bitter aftertaste. Best drunk at 12°C/54°F.

Fiano di Avellino is an elegant dry wine that goes well with all fish dishes. Serve chilled at 8°C/46°F.

Greco di tufo comes from one of the oldest vineyards in Italy, and goes well with seafood and fresh fish, or makes an excellent aperitif, providing it's served chilled.

Falanghina dei Campi Flegrei (of the Grotta del Sole label) is a dry, fruity wine, best drunk at 10°/50°C.

RED WINES

Taurasi is probably the best red wine in Campania, and is recognisable by its ruby redness. Its strong bouquet makes it an ideal accompaniment to red meat. It should be served at 18-20°C/64-68°F.

Per'e Palummo is the only red wine from Ischia. It has a warm and perfumed taste with a fruity bouquet and velvety body that goes well with both red and white meat (18°C/64°F).

Gragnano is a dark red wine with a faded violet bouquet and mellow taste. It's a slightly sparkling wine, usually drunk with white meat or a dessert (14°C/57°F).

DOG (*denominazione di origine controllata e garantita*, or guaranteed appellation contrôlée), followed by DOC (*denominazione di origine controllata*, or appellation contrôlée) and IGT (*indicazione geografica tipica*, or vin de pays).

Enoteca Partenopea
Viale Augusto, 2 (not on map)
☎ 081 593 79 82
Mon.-Sat. 10am-1.30pm, 4.30-8pm, closed 1-25 Aug.

This is one of the largest *enoteche* in the region, and has been run by Antonio Russo for over 25 years. It's located alongside the San Paolo stadium in Fuorigrotta. It's a temple to wine and contains no less than 3,000 different labels, arranged on wooden shelves by country and region of origin. In total, there are 300m²/3,250sqft of display space, and the family, who are constantly experimenting to see which wines go best with which dishes, holds several wine-tasting events a year.

Limone
Piazza S. Gaetano, 72 (C1)
☎ 081 29 94 29
Every day 10am-2pm, 4-8pm, cl. fortnight in Aug.

You'll find this shop right in the centre of the historic city. Its appeal is two-fold. Not only does it offer a vast choice of *limoncello* (a lemon liqueur in amusingly-shaped bottles (L15,000/50cl), you'll also be given an opportunity of a guided tour of the premises to see how it's produced.

Enoteca del Buon Bere
Via M. Turchi, 13 (C3)
☎ 081 764 78 43
Mon.-Sat. 9.30am-1.30pm, 4.30-8pm, cl. fortnight in Aug.

This *enoteca* was set up in 1986, the year of the Italian methanol-in-wine scandal, and so its name (roughly, the 'Good Drink Wine Bar') is no coincidence. It offers a vast selection of foreign and Italian wines that are excellent value for money. A wide range of foodstuffs, such as foie gras, charcuterie, sweets and cakes, are also sold.

OPEN-AIR MARKETS

Like many Mediterranean cities, Naples can sometimes seem like one big open-air bazaar, and street life is certainly lively. Each part of the city has its own street market. Some are fairly basic and mostly sell food. Others are smarter and more specialised. They're interesting places simply to stroll and look around, or to try to find a bargain and avoid paying over the odds. As long as you like crowds, colours, smells and noise, this very authentic side of Naples is one you'll enjoy.

Porta Nolana
Every day 8am-2pm.

The Porta Nolana market (D1), beyond the twin towers, is the best fish market in Naples. Just brought in by the fishermen, and all laid out in trays, are all kinds of shellfish, squid and other fish, some still alive, and regularly sprayed to keep them as fresh as possible. At Christmas, you'll also see tubs of still-wriggling *capitone*, a kind of large eel eaten during the festivities.

Mercatino San Pasquale
**Via S. Pasquale (B2)
Mon.-Sun. 9am-2pm.**

Unlike Porta Nolana, San Pasquale is a smart part of Naples. The market here offers attractive displays of food and clothing (more expensive here than in the centre), and is known for its 'designer' bags. However, though the prices may seem enticing, the bags are all fakes.

La Torretta
**Mergellina (not on map)
Every day 9am-1pm.**

La Torretta, in Mergellina, is one of the city's few covered markets. It's a charming place where you'll find mozzarella, beans and *friarelli* (a green vegetable that only grows in Campania), as well as slippers and embroidered clothes.

Small local markets
Mon.-Sat. 8am-1pm.

The smaller local markets are well worth a visit, and you'll generally find a mix of food, household articles, and new and

secondhand clothes. The most popular are the S. Antonio Abate (D1), la Sanità (C1), and la Pignasecca (C2), which take their names from the streets where they're held. The Fuorigrotta food market appeals to food-lovers as it offers unusually good value for money, but it's a little out-of-the-way, as are the markets in Antignano and Vomero.

Mercato del Casale di Posillipo
Parco Virgiliano (B2)
Thu. 8am-2pm.

This weekly market is held in the attractive setting of a tree-lined avenue. It sells mainly clothes, and is a good place to pad out your wardrobe. The market-goers here tend to be middle-class Neapolitans, and it's not uncommon to spot a famous face (a recent Italian president was known to shop here whenever he was on holiday in Naples).

La Duchesca
Piazza Garibaldi (D1)
Every day 9am-1pm.

Held behind the statue of Garibaldi near the station, this market sells hi-fis, cameras, TVs and camcorders. They also have excellent-quality fake Levis.

Mercato dei Fiori
Piazza Municipio (C2)
Every morning at dawn.

This flower market (which is also wholesale market) is held in the moat of the

Castel Nuovo, close to the embarkation point for the islands. This is where the city's many street vendors come to buy their supplies at dawn, a time when the city is still asleep and the soft perfumed atmosphere must be a delight. It's a lovely way to start the day and something early risers might consider.

BEWARE OF RIP-OFFS

Do be careful at the Duchesca market – you may find the absurdly cheap camcorder isn't quite what it seems when you get home. The streetwise *imbroglioni* (swindlers) who work here are perfectly capable of switching your precious purchase in front of your very eyes and replacing it with some neatly-wrapped bricks. They have years of experience, and there's no form of redress as such purchases are, of course, illegal in the first place.

Ponte di Casanova
Mon.-Sat.
8am-sunset.

The city's small flea markets are held in the area around the central station, and are often the only attraction in these rundown areas. However, flea markets in Naples are nothing like those in Paris or Rome. The Ponte Casanova market (D1) sells mainly unsold shop stock and army surplus. The Corso Malta market (not on map, near the Naples ring road) is only open on Sunday mornings, and sells secondhand items, as well as an unusual assortment of spare parts.

ANTIQUES AND SECONDHAND GOODS

The furniture and other items on sale in the shops listed below serve as a sort of piecemeal reminder of the city's glorious, but troubled history. The antique shops and secondhand dealers are all tightly packed into three specialised districts – the Jewish ghetto and along Via D. Morelli and Via S. Maria di Costantinopoli. A search for any kind of special object, whether ancient or unusual, should start here.

M. Brandi

Via D. Morelli, 9/11 (B3)
☎ 081 764 38 82
Mon.-Sat.
10am-1.30pm, 4.30-8pm.

Maurizio Brandi is the leading 18th-century specialist in Naples, and has a surprising variety of furniture and paintings. He also has some fine examples of early 19th-century French marbles, bronzes and wallpaper.

Bachelite

Vico Belledonne a Chiaia, 2 (B2)
☎ 081 41 18 60
Mon.-Sat.
10am-1.30pm, 4.30-8pm.

Bachelite is owned by Signor

Santoricho, an architect who offers his fellow Neapolitans some original ideas with which to furnish their homes. He specialises in objects from the Art Nouveau period to the 1950s, all guaranteed to provide that little extra touch of elegance to a home.

Sessantasei

Via Bisignano, 48 (B3)
☎ 081 40 15 08
Mon.-Sat.
10am-1.30pm, 4.30-8pm.

For some time this shop was located at number 'sixty-six' in the same street and has retained this number as its name. It's run by two partners, who divide their time between sales and research, particularly into 18th and 19th-century Italian and

Neapolitan painting and furniture. The displays extend over three floors, and the owners are always very helpful.

Tulli Erie

Via Bisignano, 57 (B3)
Rampe Brancaccio, 5 (B2)
☎ 081 40 00 31
Mon.-Sat.
10am-1.30pm, 4.30-8pm.

Tulli specialises in Art Deco, Liberty and Neapolitan art. She's always on the lookout for old ceramics, attractive carpets and old fabrics to please her regular clientele. Only here will you find San Leucio silk, an early 20th-century Sautto

QUAGLIOZZA

Via S. Biagio dei Librai, 11 (C1)
Mon.-Fri. 10am-2pm, 4-7pm, Sat. morning.

The steps of the church of S. Nicola a Nilo are no longer the refuge of thieves. As an inscription points out, they've been officially 'deconsecrated'. For many years now, this is where the affable Salvatore has set up his bric-a-brac stall selling lamps, mirrors, vases and glass jewellery (from L1,000). When it's busy, just follow the instructions on his notice, 'Please take a basket and help yourselves'.

Liberale rocking-chair, or a 1921 statue by the Calabrian artist Saverio Gatto, all at reasonable prices.

M & M

Via D. Morelli, 53 (B3)
☎ **081 764 40 27**
Mon.-Sat.
10am-1.30pm, 5-8pm.

M & M is so small that each object, from collectors' models of saints and porcelain to gouaches and jasper inkwells, needs to be carefully and elegantly displayed. And because space is so restricted, 18th and 19th-century furniture and paintings are on show 100m/yd further down the street at Via Vannella Gaetani, 12-15.

Bowinkel

Piazza dei Martiri, 24 (B3)
☎ **081 764 43 44**
Mon.-Sat.
10am-1.30pm, 4.30-8pm.

Bowinkel was founded in 1879 and has since become a benchmark in *belle arti* and handmade picture frames (in burr, ebony and rosewood). There's an impressive collection of objets d'art – engravings, period photographs, watercolours and attractive bronzes – at affordable prices. Ernesto, the owner, is a man renowned for his courtesy.

Fratelli Mellino

Piazzetta Nilo, 18-19 (C2)
☎ **081 552 06 30**
Mon.-Fri. 8am-7.30pm, Sat. 8am-1pm.

Fratelli Mellino sells antique and secondhand goods, and is well known in the area for the

enormous *Befana* witch that sits by the door. It's not for sale, as it's also the shop mascot. Instead, there's a range of Vietri and Umbrian ceramics (decorated with views of Naples and scenes from daily life, often featuring traditional tradespeople), as well as gouaches and furniture.

Flea market

Via Caracciolo (B3)
Sat.-Sun.

One weekend a month, the secondhand dealers show their

wares on Via Caracciolo, a street that runs alongside the seafront. It's worth going to if you have the opportunity, not least because you can combine a pleasant stroll with a rummage through the stalls. The exact dates of the market are published monthly in *Qui Napoli* (see p. 32).

LITTLE EXTRAS

Neapolitans have never lacked imagination. If proof were needed, have a look at the following businesses, which include a jeweller's, a haberdasher's, a perfumer's and a tattoo studio, some of which have only recently opened, while others have been trading for over a century.

Valù Bijoux

Vicoletto Belledonne a Chiaia, 15 (B2)
☎ 081 41 00 46
Mon.-Sat. 10am-1.30pm, 4.30-8pm.

Valentina Pianese decorated this delightful shop herself, and this is where she displays her own jewellery designs, including bracelets, rings and necklaces. The designs are all original, and forgo gold in favour of delicate and colourful materials, such as minerals from the seabed, river pearls, coral and seashells (from L120,000-800,000).

Del Porto

Via S. Lucia, 165 (C3)
☎ 081 764 00 93
Mon.-Sat. 9.15am-1pm, 4.30-7.30pm.

Alessandro, the most recent heir to a long family tradition, will explain how an object made of tortoiseshell, once considered a luxury item, is now rapidly becoming a thing of the past, and well on its way to being an antique. The lovely bracelets on display (from L250,000) all predate the 1972 international convention that ratified the protection of turtles. Along with the cigarette holders (from L90,000) and cases from the beginning of the century, you'll find coral jewellery.

Rinaldini

Via S. Biagio dei Librai, 44 (C1)
☎ 081 26 53 67
Mon.-Sat. 10am-1.30pm, 4.30-8pm.

Religion may be a serious business in Naples, but that doesn't mean it can't have a hint of humour. Take for example the holograms in which Christ gives you a friendly wink, or turns into the Virgin Mary. In fact, this shop is packed with rather more respectful holy objects, such as rosaries, medals, crucifixes and icons, as well as car-stickers.

Tramontano Bottoni

Via Chiaia, 193 (B2)
☎ 081 41 52 27
Mon.-Sat. 10am-1.30pm, 4.30-8pm.

This tiny, charming shop is completely decorated in the Liberty style, from its display window to the smallest drawer. It's here that for over a century the Tramontano family has been selling all kinds of buttons and buckles, scarves and 'things made from feathers' (L90,000/m/yd – you'll need about 1.50m/yd for a halfway decent boa).

Codrington

Via Chiaia, 94 (B2)
☎ 081 41 82 57
Mon.-Sat. 10am-1.30pm, 4.30-8pm.

Hemingway and Sophia Loren have been here before you. This unusual shop opened under the Chiaia bridge in 1886, and bizarrely brings together ornaments for the kitchen, corkscrews, cleaning products and teas, all on show in the large display windows in no particular order.

Evaluna

Piazza Bellini, 72 (C2)
☎ **081 44 57 59**
Mon.-Sat. 10am-2pm, 5pm-midnight.

Evaluna is far from being just another bookshop. For a start, it specialises in women's issues, and, secondly, Lia Polcari organises regular exhibitions, meetings and book launches. It's an inviting place, ideal for hunting out something uniquely Neapolitan, as well as for browsing through books and magazines about Naples.

essences, and perfumes unavailable elsewhere (from L100,000) – in case you're looking for something a little out of the ordinary.

Sagan

Via Filangieri, 70 (B2)
☎ **081 40 17 01**
Mon.-Sat. 9.30am-2pm, 4.30-8pm.

The window display is intriguing – the shiny silver boxes and small bottles all tied with pink ribbons hardly provide a clue as to their contents. It's only when you step inside the

Ostuni perfumes

Via V. Colonna, 39 (B2)
☎ **081 764 39 03**
Mon.-Sat. 9am-2pm, 4-8pm.

For over 50 years now, Ostuni has been one of the best places to come for perfumes, especially for more unusual fragrances. It sells

shop and breathe in the sweet, musky fragrance of perfumes created by Bruno Scamfora (L120,000 for a 5gm/^{1}/4oz phial) that you find out.

Tattoo

Calata S. Marco, 24 (C2)
☎ **081 551 10 18/
081 551 87 36**

Mon.-Sat. 10.30am-1.30pm, 4-8.30pm.

Geppi Serra can provide you with an enduring souvenir of Naples. He'll be proud to tell you that his (impeccably hygienic) tattoo studio is the only one of its kind in Southern Italy. If you aren't sure what lasting impression to have of the city, he has thousands of designs to choose from.

Il Fuso e la Forchetta

Via Pacuvio, 21 (A3)
☎ **081 714 26 17**
(groups of 10 people, by appointment).

Flavia Squillace is an outgoing and enthusiastic cookery teacher whose lessons are held in a huge kitchen overlooking the sea. They cost L80,000 a day (10am-6pm, with a half-day option available), and focus on teaching the secrets of simple and original Neapolitan recipes. Students are invited to try the results for themselves. Not all lessons are in Italian, phone for more information.

Nightlife Practicalities

Neapolitan nightlife is brilliant. Have a drink in one of the many *locali* (bars) – they have bags of atmosphere, and many have live bands. In summer, there are music festivals in and around Naples. The city doesn't sleep at weekends or during the summer season. You can lounge around with friends on a café terrace, dance the night away in an open-air nightclub, or take in a concert by the sea, and finish by greeting the dawn with a *caffé* and *cornetto*.

LISTINGS AND TICKETS

Neapolitans rarely eat much before 9pm, which is usually the time shows begin. To know exactly what's on, consult the local papers (*Mattino* and *Città*), or the Neapolitan section of a national paper (such as *Repubblica*), or buy the monthly listings magazine *Fuoribattuta* (available from record stores). You'll also need to learn to decipher the walls of the city. Many *locali* and cultural associations put up posters to advertise special events. It's relatively easy to find tickets, even at the last minute, unless the event has been heavily publicised in the media. Tickets can be bought either from Box Office (Galleria Umberto, 1 ☎ 081 551 91 88) or from Concerteria (Via M. Schipa, 23 ☎ 081 761 12 21). The agency charges commission of just under 10% of the ticket price.

NIGHTCLUBS AND *LOCALI*

Many locali are, technically speaking, cultural associations, which is why you'll need to take out a *tessera* (membership card), which is usually inexpensive (L10,000-15,000) and includes admission, though rarely a first drink. Drinks prices vary, of course, from place to place, but are usually between L10,000 and L20,000. On evenings when there's live music, and in most nightclubs, admission costs L25,000-30,000 and includes a first drink. The smarter nightclubs expect you to look decent. The number of people allowed in is sometimes limited for safety reasons, so it's best to get in before the Neapolitans, who usually arrive around 1am. You could try to reserve a table, though not all nightclubs take bookings. The fashion in nightclubs can change overnight, so ask the advice of someone who looks as if they might know.

CONCERTS

Naples has a rich music scene. The Scarlatti and Santa Caterina di Siena associations regularly arrange concerts of a high standard, the San Carlo runs a season of opera in winter performed by international singers, and sacred music concerts are given in the magnificent churches in the centre of Naples. In summer there are classical music and jazz concerts and various festivals outside Naples. Many are held in charming settings, such as the cloisters in Caserta and Aversa. International music festivals are held along the Amalfi coast in summer, including the Wagnerian opera festival staged in the magnificent cloister of Villa Rufolo in Ravello, or the Estate Musicale Sorrentina in the cloister of San Francesco.

WHERE TO GO

Where you go depends partly on when you're visiting Naples. Some cafés and nightclubs aren't open all the year. Some of the cafés in the historic centre that are packed from autumn to spring are closed in June. If this is the case, eat at one of the terraces in Piazza Bellini, or have an ice cream at the 'chalets' in Mergellina. On your way, you'll pass by some of the meeting places popular with young Neapolitans – Piazza Sannazzaro, Piazza Amedeo, Piazza del Gesù and Piazza San Domenico Maggiore – where young people gather to chat and mingle before setting off to their favourite nightclubs.

FARE UN GIRO

Fare un giro means taking a turn, going for a stroll or a drive. If you happen to fancy a change of scene, try riding out to Marechiaro for a drink to the sound of the waves lapping on the seashore. Alternatively, go up to the San Martino esplanade to watch a few a friendly football matches or wander around the harbour terraces of the Borgo Marinara. All make for a very pleasant way to spend an evening out in the soft Neapolitan night air.

Summer is the time people normally choose to go further afield to *locali* outside the centre of Naples. Popular spots among the small towns and villages in the Phlegraean Fields include the terrace of the Michelemmà, the Arenile of Bagnoli for open-air concerts and nightclubs, such as the Damiani, which has a swimming pool. Down on the more cosmopolitan Amalfi-Sorrento coast you can dance the night away under the stars and cool off with a dip in the sea. Then you can come back refreshed to Naples for another day of sightseeing or shopping in the city.

TRENDY SPOTS ALONG THE COAST

Among the many establishments along the coast, here are a few fashionable addresses: In Sorrento, Kalimera, Fauno Notte Club, Mela 2, Filou Club and Kankan. In Amalfi, Sharazad Club, Risacca di Atrani and Africana di Praiano. In Positano, Music on the Rocks, De Martino and La Bucca di Bacco.

NIGHTLIFE

When day draws to a close over the Naples of *O sole mio* and countless picture postcards, *Naples by Night* takes over. A completely different Naples comes to life – a city of concerts, nightclubs, pubs and ever-changing fashions. Whether in summer or winter, you'll be spoilt for choice in this magical city.

LIVE MUSIC

Officina 99

Via Gianturco, 101
(not on map)
Open in the evening for concerts and events.

This is the oldest and most dynamic of the occupied social centres in Naples. It's located in the industrial area to the west of the city, and can be reached by metro (get off at Gianturco). Now that it has severed its links with the local authorities, the centre runs itself and serves as a kind of showcase for both established and unknown local talent. The bar has a terrace and is an ideal place for a drink in summer.

Otto Jazz Club

Salita Cariati, 23 (B2)
☎ 081 552 43 73
Open in evening from 10pm.

The Otto Jazz Club is a cultural association funded by the Naples city council to promote jazz

music and musicians in Campania. It's popular with jazz lovers, but also music lovers in general, as the programme isn't exclusively jazz. It's very close to Corso V. Emanuele and has a bar that also serves food.

Arenile di Bagnoli

Via Coroglio, 10/14 B
(not on map)
☎ 081 230 30 50
Open 15 May-15 Oct.

Until recently, you'd never have dreamt of visiting Arenile at any time of year, let alone summer.

Five years ago, the Arenile formed part of one of Italy's largest steelworks. Since then this excellent example of land conversion has become a kind of 24-hour holiday village – where you can sunbathe and swim (L8,000 for the beach), listen to music in the evenings when there are concerts, eat local specialities and then dance the night away.

Notting Hill Gallery

Piazza Dante, 88 A (C1)
☎ 081 554 08 39
Open Oct.-May
10.30pm-5am, closed Mon.

This is an establishment with a marked preference for all things London, both in the music it plays and in the groups that are

invited to perform. You might deduce as much from the Union Jack flying above the entrance. No membership card is needed for these basement premises, unlike most other *locali*, but you do have to buy a drink (L10,000-15,000). This is where the so-called 'underground' Neapolitans come on nights when there's live music (Tue., Thu. and Sat.).

Tari Café

Via F. de Sanctis, 16 (next to the Cappella San Severo-C1)
☎ **081 251 41 15**
Open 9pm-2.30am,
closed Mon.

Behind the monumental wooden entrance is a small bar open only in summer. Throughout the rest of the year, the action is in the basement. A spiral staircase leads down to a vaulted cellar, where people come for the music. Thursday night is ethnic night, featuring food and music from the country in question. There's an entrance charge, and drinks cost L5,000-8,000.

Bogart Club

Via S. Pasquale a Chiaia, 53 (B2)
☎ **081 40 61 93**
Open every day except Monday from 8.30pm, closed May-Sep.

People usually describe the Bogart Club with adjectives such as inviting, cosy and private. The music here is mostly jazz (traditional and modern), but there are occasional exceptions. The Bogart has more recently also begun to offer good-quality cooking. You can find all this under the steely gaze of the star of *Casablanca*, who looks down at you from his portrait on the wall.

Jasay Nightlife

Via Marina, (D2) opposite the BRIN municipal car park (L500 an hour).
☎ **081 553 91 89**
Open every day exc. Mon. 9.30pm-4am, closed May-Sep.

This is the latest of the *locali alternativi*. It opened in October 1998, and is in some ways

symbolic. Located midway between the historic centre and the suburbs of Naples, it's intended to inject new life into the rundown port area, and allow those who live in different parts of the city to meet. Concert entry costs L15,000-25,000, and includes a free drink.

Michelemmà Club

Via Campana, 12, Pozzuoli (off the ring road)
☎ **081 526 97 43.**

It would be hard to find any true *uccelli di notte* (literally, 'night bird') who has not spent at least one night here. It's a concert hall and disco but also has a restaurant and pizzeria. Its theme nights are legend. In summer the delightful orange and lemon plantations in the centre of Pozzuoli draw the crowds.

DANCING

Chez Moi

Via Parco Margherita, 13 (not on map)
☎ **081 40 75 26**
Open Fri.-Sat. 11.30pm-4am, closed May-Sep.

Chez Moi has been a regular rendezvous of Neapolitan nightlife for 30 years. It's a nightclub, but with all the features you might expect from a private club – a tiny dance floor ideal for dancing cheek-to-cheek, small lounges away from the noise with waitress service and red armchairs on a midnight-blue carpet, all in all a very relaxed atmosphere for an enjoyable

evening. Entry is free but you're expected to buy a drink (L30,000).

La Mela

Via dei Mille, 40 bis (B2)
☎ **081 41 02 70**
Open Thu.-Sun. mid.-4am.

This is the most exclusive nightclub in Naples, and has been

running for over 30 years, Expect to see someone standing at the door deciding who can and can't come in. The owner, Antonello Fabbrocini, is proud to welcome Naples' smart set to his premises (the club's name means 'The Apple', a reference to New York). People come to dance (to the rhythms of Marcantonio, the resident DJ), and sometimes to attend fashion shows or book launches. Entrance, which includes a first drink, costs L30,000.

Virgilio Club

Via T. Lucrezio Caro, 6
(not on map)
☎ **081 575 52 61**
Open Wed., Fri. and Sat.
11pm-4am in summer,
closed for a fortnight in Aug.

If you suffer from claustrophobia, you'll have a great time at the Virgilio as it's the only disco in the city to have its own outdoor dance floor. It's lodged up amid the vegetation of the Vir-

giliano park, on the slope of the Posillipo, and has its own very big car park. It's also large enough to contain both the disco and a piano bar. Entrance and a free drink is L25,000.

Velvet Underground

Via Cisterna dell'Olio, 11
(C2)
Open 11am-dawn, closed
Jun.-Sep.

The Velvet (right behind the Modernissimo cinema) is many things – disco, late bar and concert hall – and should satisfy everyone, as it plays

jazz, reggae, rap and funk, as well as house, garage and hip hop. On top of this, there are also concerts by the best Italian underground bands. Membership is required (L15,000).

My Way

Via Cappella Vecchia,
30 (B3)
☎ **081 764 47 35**
Open Thu.-Sat. 10pm-4am,
closed May-Sep.

My Way is located in the very heart of the old Jewish ghetto, just a stone's throw from Piazza dei Martiri, and opens only three nights a week. As it's built into the rock, its dance floor is situated at the base of a natural cave. The DJ usually looks out over a young 20s-30s crowd.

Up Stroke

Via Coroglio, 128
(not on map)
☎ 081 570 89 92
Open Oct.-May every day
exc. Mon. 10.30pm-4am.

Since the days ten years ago
when it catered for lovers of jazz
and blues, the Up Stroke has
come a long way. Nowadays, it
even has its own recording
studio. It's usually packed at
weekends and on concert
nights, and it's best to reserve
by telephone if you want to be
sure of a table.

HAVING A DRINK

Intra Moenia

Piazza Bellini, 70 (C2)
☎ 081 29 07 20
Open 10-2am.

This was one of the first lite-
rary cafés in Naples. You can
sit, read or discuss on the terrace in summer and under the
veranda in winter. By day, it's
popular with visitors, and by
night with fashionable Neapolitans. It's an easy place to like
– not just for the attentiveness
of the waiters but also for the
setting and the wisteria, which
flowers in June.

Assultan Bar

Piazza Bellini, 64 (C2)
☎ 081 552 91 04
Open all year
8pm-3am.

Ahlan wa Sahlanî ('welcome')
to Naples' first Arabian bar,
run by Cinzia and Majed. The
Assultan attracts a varied clientele, as well as many of lthe foreign students studying in

Naples. You can have something to eat here at almost any
time of day, and at the same
time gain an insight into
Iranian and Palestinian
cuisine.

Vineria del Centro

Via Paladino, 8 A (C2)
Open Mon.-Sun.
8.30pm-3am
closed Aug.

This popular spot has been
open for 12 years, and is very
close to Piazzetta Nilo. The
music is always loud, though
it doesn't stop the clientele
from talking inside or even
outside in the street (glass in

hand, of course). There's a
room upstairs for those who
insist on sitting down, which is
sometimes also used for exhibitions.

Sly Discobar

Via Orazio, 75
(not on map)
☎ 081 66 40 48
Open Thu.-Sun. 9pm-2am,
closed May-Sep.

The Sly Discobar started as
a bet between friends who
wanted to open the perfect
bar. After a good deal of sear-
ching, they found 400m^2
/4,300sq ft of space, which they
refurbished in a warm and
welcoming style. The focal
point is the bar – both for its
reflective counter, and for the
two barmen who prepare the
sly and the *fuoco di passione*
– two blue and white cocktails
in the colours of Naples
(L15,000).

This is a good place to stop for a rest in the shade of the parasols away from the traffic, after visiting the convent of Santa Maria la Nova. There's also a good choice of local culinary specialities (lunch for L15,000-40,000, all included), and for night owls there are concerts three nights a week on the piazza in the summer.

Vibes Café

Largo S. Giovanni Maggiore, 26/27 (C1)
☎ **081 551 39 84**
Open Mon.-Fri. 8-3am, Sat.-Sun. 7pm-3am, closed 13-18 Aug.

Vibes Café is opposite the Institute of Oriental Studies and, unsurprisingly, is popular with students and teachers during the day. In the evening, the clientele is still young but more varied. From Thursday to Sunday, the café becomes a small concert hall, and the talented Neapolitan musician, Daniel Sepe plays every Friday.

De X Café

Piazzetta Ascensione, 26/27 (B2)
☎ **081 40 44 76**
Open every day except Tue. 8.30pm-3am.

This is not a bar for noughts and crosses enthusiasts, as its name might suggest. Instead, it's a piano bar, located at the foot of the attractive Church of the Ascension. It opened in 1984, and also has a good

Tempio di Bacco

Vico S. Domenico Maggiore, 1 (C1)
Closed Aug. (and when Gennaro is too tired!).

Thanks to the owner, Gennaro, this cellar, which was once used to make coffins, has now become a bar decorated on a fantastic theme. Its dim lighting, glass tables suspended from the ceiling by heavy chains, neo-Classical statues, collection of glasses on show on top of the aquarium and music all combine to make this *vineria* a place unlike any other.

Le Bar

Via Eldorado, 7 (C3)
Borgo Marinari
☎ **081 764 57 22**
Open every day except Mon. 7.30pm-2am.

Le Bar first opened its doors when the Borgo was still only inhabited by fishermen. It's located at the foot of the Castel dell'Ovo, opposite the largest hotels in Naples. Though the small port has changed a great deal since the hotel's early days, and is now swamped by Neapolitans and tourists alike in summer, it still retains unchanging pockets of authenticity, such as this bar where people come to have a drink and watch the moored boats shifting gently in the moonlight.

La Piazza

Piazza S. Maria la Nova, 23 (D2)
☎ **081 551 90 18/ 081 552 91 05**
Open Mon.-Fri. 9am-midnight, Sat.-Sun. from 6pm.

restaurant that stays open until 1am. The small piazza is a delightful spot to listen to music in the open air in summer.

counters by the entrance. Among other delicacies is the *buondi* (short for 'good morning' in Italian), a croissant with *nutella* filling (L2,500) usually eaten at the end of a long night.

VARIOUS

Bowling Oltremare

Viale J.F Kennedy, inside the Edenlandia (not on map)
☎ 081 62 44 44
Open every day 9am-2am.

Only someone with the dedication of Signor M. Scuotto could build a bowling alley with 20 computerised lanes in a city like Naples that lives and breathes football to the detriment of other sports. Yet his dedication has been paying off since 1972. Entrance is free, but expect to pay L7,000 for a game and L8,000 to rent a pair of shoes.

Gran Bar Riviera

Riviera di Chiaia, 181-183 (B3)
☎ 081 66 50 26
Open 24hrs every day.

Thanks to its owner, Simona Nunziata, this bar is not only popular with night owls and others, it's also one of the best patisseries in town. You'll find the best of local patisserie in the two

CONCERTS

Naples doesn't really have any large concert halls or stadia, such as you might find in London or New York, hence the fact that many bands and singers perform in theatres.

Palapartenope

Palazzo dello sport
Via Barbagallo (not on map)
☎ 081 570 00 08.

Thus huge tent may resemble a big top, but it has seats for 3,300 and room for 6,000 standing. Somewhat outside the centre, next to the Edenlandia park at Fuorigrotta, it's where the largest concerts featuring the biggest Italian and foreign stars are staged.

Teatro Augusteo

Piazzetta Duca d'Aosta (C2)
☎ 081 41 42 43.

The Teatro Augusteo is a small theatre close to the Umberto I Gallery. It's changed little since its opening in the 1920s, when it

Booking tickets

Here are two addresses for booking concert, theatre, opera and other tickets:

Box Office
Galleria Umberto, 1 (C2)
☎ 081 551 91 88
Concerteria
Via M.Schipa, 23 (A3)
☎ 081 761 12 21

was a place of entertainment for officials of the fascist regime. Since then, it's undergone many changes, including being a cinema and almost becoming a supermarket before reverting to its original function. It probably also has the best acoustics in Naples.

Teatro Bellini

Via Conte di Ruvo, 14 (C1)
☎ 081 549 96 88.

The original Teatro Bellini was inaugurated in 1864, only to burn down four years later. It was eventually rebuilt in 1887, to provide an alternative to the San Carlo theatre. The Bellini also lived through the theatre crisis of the 1970s and, after some renovation work, has returned to the forefront in the last decade or so. This is where you'll experience Neapolitan theatre at its most authentic. The façade and interior are a delight in themselves.

Conversion tables for clothes shopping

Women's sizes

Shirts/dresses

U.K	U.S.A	EUROPE
8	6	36
10	8	38
12	10	40
14	12	42
16	14	44
18	16	46

Sweaters

U.K	U.S.A	EUROPE
8	6	44
10	8	46
12	10	48
14	12	50
16	14	52

Shoes

U.K	U.S.A	EUROPE
3	5	36
4	6	37
5	7	38
6	8	39
7	9	40
8	10	41

Men's sizes

Shirts

U.K	U.S.A	EUROPE
14	14	36
$14^{1/2}$	$14^{1/2}$	37
15	15	38
$15^{1/2}$	$15^{1/2}$	39
16	16	41
$16^{1/2}$	$16^{1/2}$	42
17	17	43
$17^{1/2}$	$17^{1/2}$	44
18	18	46

Suits

U.K	U.S.A	EUROPE
36	36	46
38	38	48
40	40	50
42	42	52
44	44	54
46	46	56

Shoes

U.K	U.S.A	EUROPE
6	8	39
7	9	40
8	10	41
9	10.5	42
10	11	43
11	12	44
12	13	45

More useful conversions

1 centimetre	0.39 inches	1 inch	2.54 centimetres
1 metre	1.09 yards	1 yard	0.91 metres
1 kilometre	0.62 miles	1 mile	1. 61 kilometres
1 litre	1.76 pints	1 pint	0.57 litres
1 gram	0.35 ounces	1 ounce	28.35 grams
1 kilogram	2.2 pounds	1 pound	0.45 kilograms

This guide was written by **Pascale Froment** and **Frédéric Taboin**, who would like to thank **Claudine Galtieri, Marina Cataldo, Gaetano Castellano, Antonio Sperduto** and **Giuseppe Iaccarino**.
Translated by **Sam Richard**
Project manager and copy editor **Margaret Rocques**
Series editor **Liz Coghill**
Additional research and assistance **Vanessa Dowell, Jeremy Smith** and **Christine Bell**

We have done our best to ensure the accuracy of the information contained in this guide. However, addresses, phone numbers, opening times etc. inevitably do change from time to time, so if you find a discrepancy please do let us know. You can contact us at: hachetteuk@orionbooks.co.uk or write to us at Hachette UK, address below.

Hachette UK guides provide independent advice. The authors and compilers do not accept any remuneration for the inclusion of any addresses in these guides.

Please note that we cannot accept any responsibility for any loss, injury or inconvenience sustained by anyone as a result of any information or advice contained in this guide.

Photo acknowledgements

Inside pages
All photographs were taken by **Éric Guillot,** with the exception of the following:
Hachette: p. 10 (c.r.), 11 (b.r.), 16 (c.c., b.r.), 20 (t.r., b.r.), 21 (c.c.), 29 (t.), 104 (t.c.).
Nicolas Pascarel: p. 12 (b.l.), 13 (b.l), 17 (t.c., c.l., b.c.), 24 (c.r.), 31 (b.r.), 37 (c.l.), 43 (b.r.), 55 (t.r.), 57 (t.r.).
Visa Image-Alfredo Venturi: p. 16 (t.r.), 21 (b.l.).
Hémisphères Images-Stéphane Frances: p. 29 (b.l.).
Hoa Qui-Zefa-Baronne G.: p. 58 (b.r.).

Illustrations: Pascal Garnier

Cartography: © Hachette Tourisme

First published in the United Kingdom in 2000 by Hachette UK

© English Translation, revised and updated, Hachette UK 2000
© Hachette Livre (Hachette Tourisme) 1999

Distributed in the United States of America by Sterling Publishing Co., Inc.
387 Park Avenue South, New York, NY 10016-8810

A CIP catalogue for this book is available from the British Library

ISBN 1 84202 016 1

Hachette UK, Cassell & Co., The Orion Publishing Group, Wellington House, 125 Strand, London WC2R 0BB

Printed and bound in Italy by Milanostampa S.P.A.

If you're staying on a little longer and would like to try some new places, the following pages will provide you with a wide choice of hotels, restaurants and bars, listed by district. Though you can just turn up at the door of a restaurant and have a meal (except in the most prestigious establishments), don't forget to book your hotel several days in advance (see p. 66). Don't forget that prices given here are a guide only, and are subject to change. Enjoy your stay!

STAYING ON
A LITTLE LONGER

The following section includes a large number of hotels along the Amalfi coast that are ideal if you want to stay outside Naples. The prices shown are only intended to be indicative, and are always subject to change.

Amalfi

Cappucini Convento★★★★
Via Annunziatella, 46
☎ 089 87 18 77
🖷 089 87 18 86
Open all year.
This is probably the town's finest hotel. Once a 13th-century Capuchin monastery set into the rock high above Amalfi, it was abandoned for a long time, before undergoing complete restoration, though little of the original atmosphere has been lost. Previous illustrious guests include Richard Wagner and President Roosevelt. Both the views and the cooking are exceptional. There are 54 rooms, and doubles start at L240,000.

Luna Convento★★★★
Via P. Comite, 33
☎ 089 87 10 02
🖷 089 87 13 33.
The Luna Convento, which was once a convent, is located at the southernmost tip of the town, high above the sea. It has a magnificent Byzantine cloister and bell-tower. The hotel has been run by the Barbaro family since 1822, and guests continue to be drawn by the mild climate and beautiful views. Facilities include swimming pool, lifts, garden and garage. There are 45 rooms, from L190,000.

La Bussola★★★
Via Lungomare, 16
☎ 089 87 15 53
🖷 089 87 13 69
Open all year.
The Bussola was once a pasta factory, until it was bought by the Di Lieto family. It has 63 simple but spacious rooms, and the added advantage of being by the port and offering a residents-only sunbathing area on the cliff. A double room during the high season costs L200,000, breakfast included

Pensione Lidomare★★
Piazza Duchi Piccolomini
☎ 089 87 13 32
🖷 089 87 13 94.
Don't be surprised if you immediately feel at home in this family-run pensione – it's exactly how Maria and her daughter Eva want you to feel. Not surprisingly, the Lidomare is very popular with tourists. It's located in a quiet part of the town centre, and open throughout the year. Its 13 rooms are pleasantly furnished, and doubles cost L110,000, breakfast included.

Pensione Proto★
Salita dei Curiali, 4
☎ 089 87 10 03
The Proto is ideal for couples and families of 4 wishing to stay a few days in Amalfi. It's open throughout the year and offers economical (if somewhat basic) lodgings. Its 18 rooms all sleep either 2 or 4 people. In high season, a room for 4 people, with bathroom and breakfast included, costs L100,000.

Positano

Le Sirenuse★★★★★
Via C. Colombo, 79
☎ 089 87 53 82
🖷 089 81 17 98.
The Sirenuse supposedly takes its name from the sirens, who, after failing to seduce Ulysses, turned themselves to stone and became the Li Galli islets now to be seen opposite the hotel. The hotel is a former aristocratic residence, and its hillside position guarantees splendid views. Double rooms from L520,000.

San Pietro★★★★★
Via Laurito, 2
☎ 089 87 54 55
🖷 089 81 14 49
Open 1 Apr.-1 Nov.
This is one of the jewels of the Amalfi coast. It's partly built into the rock, and appears suspended between sea and sky. The San Pietro is just over a mile from Positano on the road to Amalfi. Its level of comfort is everything you would expect. It has a private swimming pool, tennis and private bathing facilities, and even a boat for trips to Amalfi at any time of the day or night. Doubles start at L650,000.

Palazzo Murat★★★★
Via dei Mulini, 3
☎ 089 87 51 77
🖷 089 81 14 19
Open 6 Mar.-7 Jan.
The Palazzo Murat, right by the beach, was once the summer residence of Joachim Murat, King of Naples. It now has an odd appearance as it's divided into two distinct parts, one the original 18th-century nucleus of the building, and the other added some 30 years ago. It also its own large private garden – a rarity in Positano. Double rooms in high season start from L350,000.

La Buca di Bacco★★★★
Via Rampa Teglia, 4
☎ 089 87 56 99
🖷 089 87 57 31
Open Apr.-Oct.
If you don't wish to spend your stay going up and down stairs to the beach and back, this is the place for you. The hotel overlooks the beach, and has a bar and restaurant open to non-residents. It has 53 rooms, starting at L50,000.

Pupetto★★★
Spiaggia Fornillo
☎ 089 87 50 87
🖷 089 81 15 17.
It was the father of the current owner who gave the hotel the name Pupetto ('little baby'). That little baby has now grown, but the name has remained. The hotel is a little outside Positano, which allows you to enjoy the surroundings in peace. It's located by the Fornillo beach and a path skirting the coast takes you to the centre in 10 mins. Rooms from L210,000, breakfast included.

Casa Albertina★★
Via della Tavolozza, 3
☎ 089 87 51 43
🖷 089 81 15 40.
This family house-hotel is perched on top of a rocky ridge, with 300 steps leading

down to the beach. The establishment is run by the Cinque family (grandmother Albertina does the cooking), and offers all you need for a quiet, pleasant stay. Rooms start at L180,000.

Ravello

Palumbo★★★★★
Via S. Giovanni del Toro, 16
☎ 089 85 72 44
🄵 089 85 81 33
Open all year.
This medieval villa built in the Moorish style, a 5-minute walk from Villa Rufolo and the cathedral, has retained its historic atmosphere. The panoramic views and restaurant are a delight. Half-board for two people in high season is L850,000 a day.

Caruso Belvedere★★★★
Piazza S. Giovanni del Toro, 2
☎ 089 85 71 11
🄵 089 85 73 72.
The Belvedere hotel, formerly Palazzo Afflitto, is at the end of Via S. Giovanni del Toro and shares the small piazza with a 12th-century church. A magnificent entranceway leads through into the garden (with gazebo). All 24 rooms either look onto the garden or the sea. Half-board for two in high season is from L320,000.

Sorrento

Grand Hotel Cocumella★★★★★
Via Cocumella, 7
Sant'Agnello
☎ 081 878 9 33
🄵 081 878 37 12
Open Mar.-Oct.
This former Jesuit convent on the outskirts of Sorrento is the only 5-star hotel in the village of Sant'Agnello. Previous guests include Goethe and the Italian writer Alberto Moravia. There's a lovely garden round the hotel and the 60 rooms have views onto the sea. The Cocumella has its own private beach and swimming pool. Double rooms are L370,000-500,000. Wheelchair facilities.

Grand Hotel Excelsior Victoria★★★★
Piazza Tasso
☎ 081 878 19 00
🄵 081 877 12 06.
This hotel, built directly on the rock in the town centre, consists of four distinct parts, each built in a different style. The oldest building is called La Vittoria, and the most recent (built in the 1920s) is called La Favorite. Countless celebrities have stayed here over the years, and one suite is named after the celebrated Neapolitan tenor Caruso, who spent the last months of his life here. The hotel has 106 rooms from L420,000 in high season.

Hotel Bellevue Sirene★★★★
Piazza della Vittoria, 5
☎ 081 878 10 24
🄵 081 878 10 24.
This became a hotel in the 19th century and was built on the remains of a Roman villa. With its views over Marina Grande, it's deservedly called the Bellevue ('good view') hotel. There's a private beach that can be reached by lift or via the garden. The 73 rooms, with all mod cons, start from L200,000 for a double.

Villa di Sorrento★★★
Via Fuorimura, 6
☎ 081 878 10 68.
This small hotel near Piazza Tasso is particularly well suited to a longer stay on the coast. All the rooms have en-suite bathrooms and toilets. Double rooms, breakfast included, start from L115,000 in high season.

La Minervetta★★
Via Capo, 25
☎ 081 807 30 69
🄵 081 807 30 69.
The Minervetta started life as a restaurant and only later acquired its 12 bedrooms. It has a strategic location which ensures a wonderful view over the whole town. The seafood specialities in the restaurant (open to non-residents) are especially recommended. Double rooms cost L80,000-110,000.

HOTELS

La Tonnarella★★
Via Capo, 31
☎ 081 878 11 53.
The Tonnarella is better known as a restaurant catering for wedding receptions and other celebrations, yet it does offer a selection of tastefully decorated rooms. A path leads from the hotel directly down to a small pebble beach, quite unlike the dark sand beaches usually found elsewhere on the coast. Double rooms are L80,000-140,000.

Residence Villagio Verde★★★
Via Cesarano, 12
☎ 081 807 32 58
𝐅 081 807 30 28
Open Mar.-Oct.
This holiday village, located right in the countryside is less than a mile from the centre of Sorrento, yet well away from any tourist crowds. For people enjoy self-catering holidays, the wood and brick bungalows are ideal. Rooms for up to 4 people are L80,000.

Capri

Quisisana & Grand Hotel★★★★★
Via Camerelle, 2
☎ 081 837 70 88
𝐅 081 837 60 80
Open Easter-Oct.
Even the most lavish praise fails to do justice to this hotel, that was originally founded as a sanatorium in the 19th century by an English physician called Clark. The views over the famous Faraglioni rocks are superb. There are 150 rooms, 2 swimming pools, 2 restaurants and a tennis court. Double rooms cost L450,000-650,000.

Punta Tragara★★★★
Via Tragara, 57
☎ 081 837 08 44
𝐅 081 837 77 90
Open Easter-Oct.
As an engraved plaque shows this historic building (formerly Villa Vismara) was designed by Le Corbusier in the 1920s. Both Eisenhower and Churchill stayed here during World War II, when it was used as a head-quarters for the American Army. There are 47 rooms,

2 swimming pools and 2 restaurants. Double rooms cost L350,000-430,000.

La Palma★★★★
Via V. Emmanuele, 39
☎ 081 837 01 33
𝐅 081 837 69 66
Open all year.
At the start of the 19th century, a lawyer by the name of Don Giuseppe Pagano decided to convert his house into Capri's first inn, at a time when the island was still relatively inaccessible. Nowadays, the inn has become a first-class hotel, and while the palm that gave the establishment its name may have disappeared, the genuine hospitality hasn't. 74 rooms from L420,000.

La Scalinatella★★★★
Via Tragara, 8
☎ 081 837 06 33
𝐅 081 837 82 91
Open 15 Mar.-end Oct.
The beautiful entrance immediately makes you want to step inside. The terrace with its swimming pool has one of the most beautiful views of the island. This luxury hotel has 30 comfortable rooms with all mod cons, its own garden and a restaurant (only open in the morning). Double rooms from L420,000.

Gatto Bianco★★★
Via V. Emmanuele, 32
☎ 081 837 02 03
𝐅 081 837 80 60
Open Easter-Nov. and Christmas holidays.
Although right in the heart of the village, and only a stone's throw away from noisy Piazza Umberto, the Gatto Bianco has achieved the impossible and is actually surprisingly peaceful. Since it doesn't have a restaurant of its own, arrangements have been made with 7 of the islands' restaurants where you can have dinner for L40,000. There are 37 rooms, doubles from L180,000.

Villa Sarah★★★
Via Tiberio, 3 A
☎ 081 837 78 17
𝐅 081 837 72 15
Open end Mar.-Oct.

Its situation in one of the higher parts of the island, on the road leading to Villa Jovis, means that Villa Sarah benefits from superb panoramic views and particularly agreeable temperatures in summer. Set in its own private garden, it feels more like one of Capri's private villas than a hotel. There are 20 rooms, and singles are L110,000.

Quattro Stagioni★
Via Marina Piccola
☎ 081 837 00 41
Open Apr.-Oct.
This is an address often found in budget travel guidebooks, as the Quattro Stagioni offers excellent value for money. The hotel is located at the beginning of the road leading directly to Marina Piccola. The standard of hospitality is high, but that's what you can traditionally expect to find all over the island. It has a garden, and 11 rooms (L120,000-160,000).

Belsito
Via Matermania, 9
☎ 081 837 87 50/
081 837 09 69
𝐅 837 66 22.
This pensione really is in a fine place (a 'bel sito'), as its name suggests, as it's located on the road to the Arco Naturale and Grotta di Matermania, and has many pleasant surprises in store for you – the peace and quiet, the small balconies looking out onto the sea, the pergola or perhaps even the standard of cooking in the nearby restaurant. Double rooms start from L80,000.

Villa Krupp★★
Viale G. Matteotti, 12
☎ 081 837 03 62
𝐅 081 837 64 89
Open all year.
The German steel magnate Alfred Krupp loved Capri – even though the inhabitants of the island weren't prepared to let him buy it. This establishment is a villa (taking its name from the magnate's former residence nearby) that's delightful for its peaceful, unassuming charm – on an island where by now much has been sacrificed to mass tourism. The 12 rooms offer views over the sea and the Faraglioni. L160,000-210,000.

La Tosca★
Via D. Birago, 5
☎ 081 837 09 89
Open Apr.-Oct.
La Tosca is a little outside the centre of fashionable Capri, and people come here for its peace and serenity. It's in the kind of setting you see families coming out for a stroll in the cool late-afternoon air. Access to La Tosca is along a path. There are 12 rooms, double rooms are L100,000.

Antonino Vuotto
Via Campo di Teste, 2
☎ 081 837 02 30
Open all year.
These guestrooms (doubles), are right next to Via Camerelle and all the luxury hotels. A convenient place to stay for a night on the island.

Salvatore Catuogno
Via D. Birago, 1
☎ 081 837 01 28
Open in summer.
These are guestrooms (doubles), all with en-suite bathroom and south-facing balcony. Prices start from L70,000.

Anacapri

Caesar Augustus★★★★
Via Orlandi, 4
☎ 081 837 14 21
📠 081 556 01 19.
The hotel's name is a homage to one of the island's most illustrious visitors – Emperor Augustus, whose statue adorns the terrace. The emperor (who had more than one residence on the island) would certainly have appreciated the dramatic view down to the sea below. The level of comfort leaves nothing to be desired. 58 rooms, some with a small living room, from L180,000.

Biancamaria★★
Via G. Orlandi, 54
☎ 081 837 13 60
📠 081 837 20 60
Open Easter-Oct. and Christmas holidays.
The Biancamaria is most often described as a welcoming place. It looks out over the shop-lined street where the inhabitants of Anacapri stroll up and down in the evening.

The 25 rooms offer views of either the sea or Mount Solaro, and start from L150,000. There's no restaurant.

Villa Eva★
Via La Fabbrica, 8
☎ 081 837 15 49
📠 081 837 20 40
Open Mar.-Oct.
As it's one of the cheapest places to stay, Villa Eva has become well known to tourists wishing to spend several days on the island. It's also located on the road leading to the Grotta Azzurra. A double room is L60,000-70,000, not including breakfast. Reservations are a must in high season.

San Michele★★★
Via G. Orlandi, 1-5
☎ 081 837 14 42
📠 081 837 14 20.
Built at the end of the 19th century, the San Michele has retained much of ts original atmosphere. It's a stone's throw from the beach, and has about 60 rooms with views of the nearby Mount Solaro. The restaurant seats around 300, and meals cost L30,000-40,000. The hotel has its own bus link with the port. Expect to pay L180,000-220,000 for a double room.

Ischia

Grand Hotel Punta Molino★★★★★
Ischia
Lungomare Colombo
☎ 081 99 15 44
📠 081 99 15 62.
Located 15 minutes from the town centre, this prestigious 5-star hotel complex has everything you might want – private beach, restaurant with panoramic vie.v, thermal baths, beauty salon, two swimming pools (one indoors) and more besides. Double rooms start at L500,000.

Hotel Terme Continental★★★★
Ischia
Via M. Mazzella, 60
☎ 081 99 15 88
📠 081 98 29 29.
This is the kind of establishment that has so much to offer its guests that some probably

HOTELS

never leave its confines. You can even do your shopping here. Rooms are in charming little villas or small Mediterranean-style blocks. The hotel offers a bus service to the beach. Doubles from L190,000.

Pensione Il Monastero★★

Ischia:
Castello Aragonese
☎ 081 99 24 35.
The Pensione Il Monastero is the ideal place to soak up the medieval atmosphere of the rocky Castello Aragonese promontory. It's only a few minutes from the town centre, yet well away from the noise and has a wonderful view of the castle as well. There are 14 rooms, with doubles starting at L110,000.

Camere da Sabine

Ischia:
Via Campagnano, 20 H
☎ 081 90 11 79
Open all year.
Camere da Sabine offers bed and breakfast alongside the Castello Aragonese for only L25,000-30,000. It's an ideal place to stay for a night, and offers views of the Bay of Naples as far as Sorrento. Popular with students and others on a budget from all over the world.

Il Vitigno

Forio:
Via Bocca, 31
☎ 081 998 307
Open all year.
This rural gîte is the only farm on Ischia that also offers self-catering facilities. It's an ideal place for nature lovers, and well situated for numerous rewarding walks. You also have an opportunity to try island-grown food, washed down with local wine. L50,000 per person, breakfast included.

Camping Mirage

Barano:
Spiaggia
dei Maronti
☎ 081 99 05 51
Open all year.
The Camping Mirage, located in the south of the island, offers 10,000m^2 of land off the attractive Maronti beach. Caravans and campers pay L11,000-13,000 a day, tents L6,500. There's a terrace-bar and restaurant.

Procida

Pensione Savoia★

Via Lavadera, 32
☎ 081 896 76 16
Open all year.
Time seems to have stood still here for many years, and that's what makes this Pensione so attractive. If you remember to ask for a room facing the sea, you'll have one of the best views on the island. L90,000 for two, breakfast included.

Hotel Casa Gentile★★

Marina Coricella, 88
☎ 081 896 77 99
✆ 081 896 90 11.
This is right by the small, charming Coricella fishing harbour, an area that has escaped mass tourism. This small pensione, quite in keeping with its peaceful surroundings, has 6 rooms, each with a terrace and sea view.

Phlegraean Fields

Albergo Al Chiar di Luna★

Monte di Procida:
Via Amedeo, 74
☎ 081 868 24 24/
081 868 21 80.
Monte di Procida and the nearby Capo Miseno form the part of the coast that closes the bay to the north. This small hotel is at the top of the hill and all the rooms have a panoramic view. When the weather is fine, breakfast is served outdoors. Double rooms cost L80,000, breakfast included.

Country Club Hotel Damiani

Pozzuoli:
S. S. Domitiana-km. 21
☎ 081 804 26 66
✆ 081 804 25 70.
This resort can make you forget the outside world as soon as you set foot inside. It's all laid on for you – sports (tennis, volleyball, basketball and go-karting) during the daytime, and restaurant, bar, and nightclub at night, with a dip in the swimming pool to freshen you up in the morning. 20 or so bungalows, L130,000 for 4 people.

Hotel Solfatara★★★

Pozzuoli:
Via Solfatara, 163
☎ 081 526 26 66/
081 526 70 17.
The Solfatara is one of the best hotels in the area. It's very strategically located – close to the metro and the centre of Pozzuoli, and close to the ring road and the sea. It's both functional and practical, and those who love the area always come here. 31 rooms, doubles from L150,000.

HOTELS

In general, the prices shown are for a full meal, not including drinks. Please bear in mind that some of the smaller and less expensive restaurants only accept cash.

Historic centre

Amici Miei★★
Via Monte di Dio, 78
☎ 081 764 60 63
Closed Sun. evening and Mon.
Around L50,000.
Regulars often pop in for a meal or a chat with the owner after seeing a show at the nearby Teatro Politeama. The choice of dishes is so varied it's hard to know what to order. A word of advice: accept suggestions.

Il Gobbetto★★
Via Sergente Maggiore, 8
☎ 081 41 14 83
Closed Sun.
Around L35,000.
If something is 'aumm aumm' in Neapolitan dialect, it means it's secret. Here in this small restaurant next to Piazza Trieste e Trento, a popular spot after the shows in the San Carlo or Augusteo theatres, you can try Maccheroncelli Aumm Aumm – though in this case, the recipe's no secret.!

Santa Lucia Borgo Marinaro

Il Posto Accanto
Via N. Sauro 2/5
☎ 081 764 86 00
Closed Sun.
L50,000-70,000.
'Il Posto Accanto' means 'the place next door', in this case, next door to the famous Rosolino restaurant. It's a cosier, less expensive and less formal version of the latter, though the same man owns both restaurants. It's a welcoming place facing out to sea, with a different menu every day.

Zi Teresa
Borgo Marinaro
☎ 081 764 25 65
Closed Mon. and Sun. evenings.
Around L60,000.

Zi Teresa, opposite some of the city's luxury hotels and facing the small port of Borgo Marinaro, offers a vast choice of fish and seafood dishes. The house speciality is Fusillo Riva Fiorita – pasta, seafood and basil. Enjoy!

Riviera

La Cantina di Triunfo★★
Riviera di Chiaia, 64
☎ 081 66 81 01
Closed Sun.
L40,000-50,000.
This isn't like other restaurants, as it was once a wine shop, and wine is still sold here in the mornings. It's an unpretentious place, offering good cooking. For once, choosing a meal shouldn't be difficult – there are only two primi (starters) and two secondi (main dishes) every evening.

Trattoria dell'Oca★
Via S. Teresa a Chiaia, 11
☎ 081 41 48 65
Closed Sun.
Set meal L20,000 (lunch)-L30,000 (even.).
At lunchtimes, the trattoria is full of regulars who come for the tasty traditional dishes. In the evenings, a more refined selection of Neapolitan and other Mediterranean dishes (which vary according to the season) is on offer. Prices are higher in the evenings, though still quite reasonable. The house speciality, a chocolate soufflé, has to be ordered at the start of the meal.

Il Canterbury
Via Ascensione, 6
☎ 081 41 16 58
Closed Sun.evening.
L15,000 (lunch)-L25,000 (evening).
Once upon a time Adamo and his future wife found themselves eating in a Parisian restaurant. During the course of the meal, Adamo told her that he'd one day like a restaurant like the one they were eating in. That day finally came, and this is the result. It offers interesting dishes, served in an inviting setting.

Umberto Pizzeria
Via Alabardieri, 30/31
☎ 081 41 85 55

This pizzeria opened in 1917 and has become a household name. The menu varies according to the season. In summer, for example, fresh toppings are added to some of the pizzas after they've been cooked. The winter menu, on the other hand, is heavier and rich in calories. The restaurant is well suited to tourists as there's live traditional Neapolitan music.

El Bocadillo★★
Via Martucci, 50
☎ 081 66 90 30
Closed Mon.
This very lively taverna has plenty of South American decor, including Inca masks and Aztec carpets. Apart from serving food, it's also a popular nightspot (you may need to raise your voice at the table). French, English, Spanish and Arabic are all spoken here.

Zorbas★★
Gradini Amedeo, 5
☎ 081 66 75 72
Evenings only
Closed Mon.
Around L35,000.
You only have to set foot in this small inn to feel as if you were on holiday in Greece or on one of the Greek islands. The menu offers various Greek specialities, listed by region, and the food is prepared by a real Greek chef.

Mergellina and Posilippo

Don Salvatore★★★
Via Mergellina, 5
☎ 081 68 18 17
Closed Wed.
Around L70,000.
The owner of this restaurant is also an expert on wines, which explains why the wine list is so long and appealing. The menu offers traditional regional specialities, updated for current tastes. It's advisable to reserve in summer.

Giuseppone a Mare★★★
Capo Posillipo
Via F. Russo, 13
☎ 081 769 13 84/
081 575 60 02
Closed Mon.
Around L70,000.

This restaurant has an exceptional view of the Bay of Naples. It also has 8 chefs, each chosen for his own speciality. The Polippo Giuseppone is particularly good – octopus cooked in an earthenware dish. Many have tried to copy this dish and failed.

A Fenestella ★★
Calata del Ponticello
a Marechiaro, 23
☎ 081 769 00 20
Closed Wed. lunchtime
and Sun. evening, and
10 days at Christmas
and a fortnight in Aug.
L70,000-80,000.
The window in this restaurant is where Carolina, a young Neapolitan girl, listened to her sweetheart serenading her below – which inspired the poet Salvatore di Giacomo to write his famous poem. The restaurant belongs to the Unione Nazionale del Buon Ricordo (National Union of Restaurants), which is obviously a good guarantee of what to expect. The Linguine al Coccio (with sea snails) are served in particularly attractive earthenware dishes.

Spaccanapoli, Montesanto and Portalba

900 Pizzeria
Via P. Scura, 5
☎ 081 552 16 34
Closed Sun.
Around L12,000.
A quick way to tell how good a place is, is to count the number of people queueing outside at the weekend. And queues at weekends outside this pizzeria, which opened at the start of the 20th century and is located between Pignasecca and Via Roma, are very long indeed.

Al 53 ★★
Piazza Dante, 53
☎ 081 549 93 72
Around L50,000.
As a starter, the chef offers a selection (misto) of 14 starters. If you're still hungry after that, succumb to the temptation of Conchiglioni alla Siciliana (aubergine/eggplant, ham and mozzarella).

Vomero

Acunzo ★
Via D. Cimarosa, 60
☎ 081 578 53 62
Closed Sun.
Around L18,000.
This pizzeria offers the whole range of traditional Neapolitan pizzas, but you can also try some of the pizzaiolo's more outlandish concoctions, such as the successful mix of pizza and macaroni. Not something that immediately springs to mind, but delicious all the same.

Gorizia
Via L. Bernini, 29
☎ 081 578 22 48
Closed Wed.
Around L15,000.
Opposite the shopping arcade is one of the oldest pizzerias in Vomero. It opened on 16 August 1916, the day of the fall of Gorizia, a town in Northern Italy, hence its name and also the name of the house speciality.

Il Gallo Nero ★★★
Via T. Tasso, 446
☎ 081 64 30 12
Closed Sun. and Mon. lunchtimes
L70,000-80,000.
This was once a wine shop selling the Chianti Classico from the famous Gallo Nero label. The restaurant is housed in a villa, accessible by lift or stairs leading up to a small, panoramic terrace. Particularly good here is the sea bream cooked Creole-style, in a lemon, white olive and white wine sauce.

Fuorigrotta

Cafasso
Via G. Cesare, 156
☎ 081 239 52 81
Closed Sun.
Around L15,000.
This pizzeria, next to Piazzale Tecchio, has long had an excellent reputation. As you wait for your pizza, try the delicious mixed antipasti (starters). The chef here has become an expert at preparing them, and your wait will pass all the more quickly.

RESTAURANTS

Phlegraean Fields

Fefè★★
Bacoli:
Via Miseno, 137
☎ 081 523 30 11
Closed Sun. evening
and Mon.
Around L40,000
In summer, Fefè is fully booked every evening of the week, and without a reservation, you're unlikely to eat before midnight. It's a pleasant place, the cooking is unpretentious and the service prompt – the kind of place people often return to. Drop by if you're in the area.

La Misenetta★★★★
Bacoli:
Via Lungolago, 2
☎ 081 523 41 69
Closed Mon. except in
summer.
Around L60,000.
This is a kind of winter garden opposite the Villa Comunale. The cook is a real believer in good food and the menu full of sophisticated and original dishes, particularly the Risotto alle Ostriche (with oysters) and the Farfalle agli Agrumi Orientali e ai Gamberi (with prawns).

Il Capitano★★
Pozzuoli:
Lungomare Colombo, 13
☎ 081 526 22 83
Closed Thu.
Around L50,000.
Once upon a time at the end of the 19th century, a captain from Calabria fell in love with a beautiful woman from Pozzouli, and instantly decided to settle here with her. They opened a small restaurant in the heart of the port in Pozzouli, where you can still find it today. A good place to eat on your way to the islands.

Capri

La Capannina
Via delle Botteghe, 12 bis
(Capri)
☎ 081 837 07 32
Closed Nov.-Easter
Around L70,000.
You should have no difficulty in finding this restaurant in Via delle Botteghe ('Street of Shops'). Far from resembling a beach hut (as its name would suggest), this looks like, and is, a traditional restaurant, except for one small detail – it has its own wine cellar. If during the meal you discover a wine you particularly like, try the Capanina wine shop further down the road, which sells local produce of the island as well (☎ 837 88 99).

Le Grottelle★★
Capri:
Via Arco Naturale, 13
☎ 081 837 57 19
Closed mid-Nov-mid-Mar.
Around L50,000.
The Grotelle is both a pizzeria and a restaurant, and is located near the Arco Naturale. The view from the terrace is magnificent. The house speciality is the famous Ravioli Capresi. Don't leave the island without trying it.

Add'o Riccio ★★★
Anacapri:
Via Grotta Azzurra, 11
☎ 081 837 13 80
Closed Nov.-Feb. and
evenings, except in
summer
Around L60,000
Try (if you can) to reach this restaurant above the Grotta Azzurra on foot. That way you'll have worked up an appetite for the seafood specialities served here. There's a commanding view of the Mediterranean from the terrace and arbour.

La Savardina★
Capri:
Via Lo Capo 8
☎ 081 837 63 00
Closed Jan.-Feb.
and Tue. except in
summer
Around L30,000.
You'll find this trattoria on the road to Villa Fersen and Punta del Capo, in one of the higher parts of the island. Here, surrounded by the orange and lemon trees in the garden, you'll discover a warm hospitality that is as generous as the portions.

Ischia

Lo Scoglio★★
Sant'Angelo:
Via Cava Ruffano
☎ 081 99 95 29
Around L50,000.

As its name suggests, this restaurant is perched on a rock high above the sea, and the view from the veranda is splendid. The specialities are fish and seafood dishes, and given the popularity of the establishment, prior reservation is essential.

Il Focolare★★
Casamicciola:
Via Cretaio, 36
☎ 081 98 06 04
Closed Wed. (except in
summer) and Mon., Wed.
and Thu. lunchtimes.
Around L50,000.
The Focolare's kitchen relies more on the island's agricultural produce than on the surrounding sea – instead of Linguine alle Vongole or Frittura di Paranza, you can order game (wild boar), beef and the well-known dish Coniglio all'Ischitana – rabbit with a sauce made from offal, white wine and small island tomatoes.

Procida

Gorgonia★★
Marina Coricella, 50
☎ 081 810 10 60
Closed Oct.-Apr.
Around L50,000.
The Gorgonia is on the far side of the small port of Coricella, and offers an intimate setting for a candlelit dinner. Fish and seafood specialities, in particular the Pasta e Fagioli con le Cozze (pasta with white beans and mussels). Absolutely delicious!

La Conchiglia
Via Pizzaco, 10
☎ 081 896 76 02
Around L40,000.
For a real taste of Procida, visit Tonino's restaurant. He specialises in what he loves – namely fish. The menu varies from one day to the next, depending on what the fishermen catch in the morning. You can expect a warm welcome, quality cooking, and a view of the port of Coricella from the shade of the pergola.

Sorrento peninsula

Caruso★★★
Sorrento:
Piazza Tasso
☎ 081 807 31 56
Closed Mon.
Around L70,000.

If you can't afford to stay at the Caruso suite in the Excelsior Vittoria, you might feel like paying your respects to the legendary tenor here, where the walls are decorated with photographs, signatures and clippings of the great man. The menu includes the delicious Ravioli alla Caruso, with cheese filling and aubergine (eggplant) sauce.

Emilia★
Via Marina Grande, 62
☎ 081 878 14 89/
081 807 27 20
Closed Tue.
Around L30,000.
In winter, meals are served in the small dining room, and in summer on the terrace right by the sea. The fish specialities (caught that morning) are prepared as they would be in many homes on the island.

Amalfi Coast

La Cambusa★★★
Positano:
Piazza Amerigo
Vespucci, 4
☎ 089 87 54 32
Closed Tue. (except in summer) and Wed.
L50,000-80,000.
Throughout the year, meals are served on the terrace that looks out to sea near the Marina Grande. It's a particularly appealing sight in winter, when there are no tourists to spoil the expanse of beach. Fish and seafood are specialities, in particular baked fish with new potatoes.

Cumpà Cosimo★★
Ravello:
Via Roma, 42-44
☎ 089 85 71 56
Closed. Mon. (except in summer)
Around L50,000.
This place was once famous as a wine shop, but it is now known for its excellent homemade cooking, hence the long and impressive list of past celebrity customers, including the likes of Humphrey Bogart and Jacqueline Kennedy. All the pasta is handmade, and the gnocchi and fusilli are particularly good here.

Don Alfonso 1890★★★★★
Piazza S. Agata, 11
☎ 089 878 00 26
Closed Mon. and Tue.
(Mon. in summer)
Around L120,000.
Don Alfonso is one of Italy's most famous restaurants. Inventive and refined dishes made with local produce, served in an elegant setting, all courtesy of Alfonso and Livia Iaccarino.

RESTAURANTS

Don't leave Naples without at least trying some of the local patisserie and ice cream. *Babà, sfogliatelle, zeppole* and many others can be eaten at any time of day. Below are the addresses of the best patisseries and ice-cream parlours in the city.

Toledo and historic centre

Augustus
Via Toledo, 147
☎ 081 551 35 40
Open every day.
Via F. Petrarca, 81 A/B
☎ 575 47 82
Closed Sun.
You must try the house speciality, the rose cake (cream, ricotta, fruits of the forest and rose petals), and the mint-flavoured Pan di Spagna. Other local specialities include the Delizie al Limone (lemon-flavoured) and the Crostatine (toasted fried bread with various savouries).

La Scimmia
Piazza Carità, 4
☎ 081 552 02 72
Closed Wed.
This was Naples' first ice-cream parlour, which opened in 1933. Stepping away from the hustle and bustle of Via Toledo and into La Scimmia always makes a very welcome break. Here you'll find all flavours of ice cream, including some very unusual ones. The cassatas (regular or with fruit) are delicious.

Cibo
Piazza del Gesù, 27
Via D. Cimarosa, 144
☎ 081 556 81 69
Open every day.
It's best to come here for the saltimbocche as the pastry is excellent and you can choose the filling – aubergines (eggplant), mushrooms, artichokes, ham or cheese. They're are a good bet if you're looking for a quick snack. However, the tavola calda leaves a little to be desired, and the variety of pizzas can't hide the fact that they're not the best.

L.U.I.S.E.
Piazza S. Domenico
Maggiore, 5
☎ 081 551 44 77
Closed Sun.
L.U.I.S.E. in San Domenico is a big improvement on the old premises in Via Toledo. It has a large terrace set out on the piazza when the weather's fine, and a quiet room indoors which is open throughout the day. Both the patisserie and the selection of ready-made dishes served at lunchtime are good. This is a pleasant place to come and eat, and one that regularly holds temporary exhibitions and concerts.

Chiaia and Mergellina

Grand Bar Riviera
Riviera di Chiaia, 183
☎ 081 66 50 26.
This café opened in 1870 and is famous for having invented, over a quarter of a century ago, the tartufo (ice-cream cake made from chocolate ice cream and chestnut cream). The Grand Bar Riviera is the ideal place to try a whole range of traditional patisserie (pastiera, zeppole, babà, sfogliatelle and others), as well as iced fresh strawberries and various granita in summer. It's open 24hrs a day, and the café specialises in early morning breakfasts, in particular doughnuts with Nutella or white chocolate filling.

Remy Gelo
Via F. Galiani, 29
☎ 081 66 73 04
Closed Mon.
Remy Gelo is one of Naples' leading ice-cream parlours and offers a whole profusion of flavours and varieties of ice cream that vary according to the time of the year. One particular masterpiece is the pastiera cornetto – the taste's so faithful to that of the original pastry you won't believe it. Or there's the ice-cream cake with strawberries and bilberries (blueberries). If you prefer a savoury snack, you can enjoy the Panyllo sandwich made with ham and cheese.

Moccia
Via San Pasquale, 21-22
☎ 081 41 13 48
Closed Tue.

Moccia has been a patisserie, ice-cream parlour and bakery for over 50 years. Aside from a selection of traditional cakes, it offers a range of typically Neapolitan specialities (freselle, taralli, etc.). The small pizzas make an excellent mid-morning or afternoon snack.

Luigi Caflisch & C
Via Chiaia, 142
Via dei Mille, 91/93
☎ 081 40 45 88.
Patisserie prepared by Luigi Caflisch was appreciated by the aristocrats at the court of the Kingdom of the Two Sicilies. The original establishment has since closed, but you can still try some exquisite examples in one of the two patisserie/cafés. The chocolates are handmade. Try the Swiss cannolletti with caramelised chestnuts. No-one could ask for more.

Vomero

Bellavia e Figli
Piazza Muzii, 27
☎ 081 558 44 76
Via O. Fragnito 82
☎ 081 546 32 98
Closed Thu.
Bellavia is particularly busy around breakfast-time, and an early-morning visit would be worth it for the brioches, croissants and grafe (delicious sweet doughnuts) alone. This is also a good place to buy Sicilian specialities (cassatas and cannoli) and all kinds of profiteroles.

Near the railway station

Carraturo
Corso Garibaldi, 59
☎ 081 554 34 44
Via V. Arangio Ruiz, 75/79
☎ 081 68 17 95.
You might want to drop in here for breakfast or a tasty snack on your way in or out of Naples as Carraturo is located opposite the Circumvesuviana railway station. Products are always fresh. Regulars come here for the cakes and Torta Carratura, a cake made with cream and profiteroles. The Carraturo on Corso Garibaldi also has a cafeteria/snack bar.